"In my own experience, the challenge of distinguishing between mental health conditions and demonization is a pressing issue that needs more thoughtful attention. I appreciate how [this book] highlights that psychological issues can sometimes accompany possession. There is a significant gap in effective teaching on this subject, and an urgent need to equip leaders to navigate these complexities. I sincerely hope [this] work fosters a more integrated approach to deliverance and counseling."

—**Darla Rakes**, Ambassador to Students and Donors, Evangel University

"Dr. Rob Willis has provided an excellent resource for pastors and ministry leaders. This text will not only fit nicely on the pastor's shelf of practical books, it will also serve as a window through which the biblical worldview is recaptured for modern leaders."

—**Darryl L. Fitzwater Jr.**, Bishop, Diocese of All Saints (ACNA)

". . . [A] very good book with both biblical/theological depth and balance and sound psychological perspectives, as well as some relevant church history and a good review of the literature on deliverance and exorcism. . . . One of the best I have read in this area of deliverance."

—**Siang-Yang Tan**, Senior Professor of Psychology, Fuller Theological Seminary

"In *The Deliverance Dialogues*, Dr. Willis shares with us years of ministry training, research, and Spirit-led direction for addressing both mental health and demonic possession. This much-needed, practical guide tackles issues the church has too often evaded, providing ministry leaders with a valuable resource to help those who have felt there was no help."

—**David Willis**, Lead Pastor, Link Church, Clarksville, Arkansas

"The call to ministry is not solely to impact the lives of people but also to engage the unseen world. This book is a practical resource that helps pastors and ministry leaders navigate the two worlds. It offers insight to discern what belongs to the realm of broken humanity and what can appropriately be attributed to spiritual forces of evil. Pentecostal practitioners will gain wisdom for the pulpit, the altar, and the counseling room."

—**Cory Shipley**, Associate Professor of Practical Theology, Assemblies of God Theological Seminary

The Deliverance Dialogues

The Deliverance Dialogues

Perspectives on Mental Illness and Demonic Influence

Robert Willis

Foreword by Carolyn Tennant

WIPF & STOCK · Eugene, Oregon

THE DELIVERANCE DIALOGUES
Perspectives on Mental Illness and Demonic Influence

Wipf & Stock
An Imprint of Wipf and Stock Publishers
199 W. 8th Ave., Suite 3
Eugene, OR 97401

www.wipfandstock.com

PAPERBACK ISBN: 979-8-3852-7835-0
HARDCOVER ISBN: 979-8-3852-7836-7
EBOOK ISBN: 979-8-3852-7837-4

VERSION NUMBER 04/02/26

To my loving wife,

Anna May.

Thank you for journeying with me on this adventure of life and for the countless hours you have invested in proofreading, listening, and encouraging me to see this project through to completion. Thank you for being my best friend and partner in ministry from the very beginning.

Contents

Foreword by Carolyn Tennant | ix
Preface | xi
Acknowledgments | xv
Introduction: From Eternia to Exorcism | xvii

Chapter 1: When a Shower Won't Fix It | 1
Chapter 2: The Clash of Kingdoms | 13
Chapter 3: The Key to Sustained Freedom | 22
Chapter 4: Echoes of Power | 32
Chapter 5: Pastors in the Crossfire | 47
Chapter 6: Degrees of Darkness | 66
Chapter 7: Pathways to Demonic Distress | 78
Chapter 8: The Intersectionality of Dissociation and Demonization | 91
Chapter 9: Healing the Divided Soul | 105
Chapter 10: Diagnosing Demonization | 117
Chapter 11: Unclean No More | 130
Chapter 12: The Journey to Freedom | 149
Conclusion: The Dragon and the Deliverer | 160

Appendix A: The Importance of Forming Therapeutic Alliances | 163
Appendix B: Ethics in Deliverance Ministry | 167
Appendix C: Demonization and Believers | 171
About The Author | 177
Sources Consulted | 179

Foreword

ONCE EVERY 15–20 YEARS in academia, we professors have the exceptional privilege of guiding an extremely intelligent and unusually insightful person through the dissertation process, and the paper is on an amazing topic as well.

Dr. Robbie Willis is just such a person. Having deep spiritual insight as well as experience with both deliverance ministry and counseling, he was ready to tackle questions regarding the intersection between mental health and demon possession.

This topic comes at a hot button moment when Wiccan and witchcraft is growing in the United States. So are mental health problems of all sorts, especially among young people. Many of us are unable to discern what the real roots and issues are for what is plaguing our friends and family members. Pastors are also facing difficulties as they counsel and seek to assist their congregations.

This book, *The Deliverance Dialogues,* puts the research from his excellent doctoral dissertation into a book that is both readable and very useful.

- If you are a pastor who has wondered when you should refer someone you are counseling to a mental health professional, this book is for you.
- If you are a pastor who has asked how you can continue pastoral counseling with someone who is under the care of a mental health professional, this book is for you.
- If you want to know how to do a better job in deliverance ministry, this book is for you.

- If you are a mental health counselor and wonder when you should refer a client to a pastor, this book is for you too.

I highly recommend that you give a few hours to read this unique book that will give you skills and knowledge to last a lifetime. You'll find it a friendly read and well worth your investment of time.

Rev. Carolyn G. Tennant, PhD
Dissertation advisor for Dr. Willis at the Assemblies of God Theological Seminary at Evangel University (Springfield, MO)

Preface

When I answered the call to preach in 1997, I had only witnessed a demon being cast out on one occasion, and I knew virtually nothing about mental illness. What I did know was that Jesus Christ had redeemed me, and I wanted to devote my life entirely to his service. Life and ministry have taken me on many unexpected twists and turns. As I prepared to leave home at the age of eighteen to attend Central Bible College, a relative asked me, "Do you really think you need to go to college to be a preacher?" I replied, "No, I don't. I come from a long line of preachers whom God has used without a Bible college education. But people give their lives to many causes. I want to give mine to understanding the Scriptures." That conviction—that God has spoken to humanity through his Word—has been my anchor in every season. It has forced me to re-examine my beliefs, refine my theology, and submit my thinking to the truth of Scripture again and again.

The Deliverance Dialogues is the culmination of nearly three decades of biblical study and personal experience in "the school of the Spirit." It is born from my sincere desire to help the hurting and the broken find freedom and healing through Jesus Christ. This work draws heavily on the research I completed as part of my doctoral journey at the Assemblies of God Theological Seminary and is written primarily with pastors and Christian counselors in mind. My prayer is that it will serve as a tool to help ministers become more discerning and effective in both assessment and intervention—without ever replacing the leadership and empowerment of the Holy Spirit.

While the primary audience is pastors and ministry leaders, this book will also be valuable for any believer who wants to help a friend or family member in distress, as well as for those who are personally seeking freedom. My focus throughout has been the pastoral counseling context. Portions of the book may strengthen a minister's effectiveness at the altar, but it is designed more as a manual for walking with people through the often long and deeply personal process of healing and deliverance.

The research behind these pages includes engagement with voices from psychiatry, clinical psychology, anthropology, pastoral ministry, and the world of exorcism.[1] I am not a mental health professional. I am a pastor—an ordained minister with the Assemblies of God—who holds certifications in trauma-informed mental health coaching and suicide prevention through the American Association of Christian Counselors. More than any of these credentials, I am a follower of Jesus Christ who believes He is still "doing good and healing all who are oppressed by the devil" (Acts 10:38).

Although I realize that the word "exorcism" may be uncommon, or even uncomfortable, for some readers, I have chosen to use it throughout this book for a particular reason. After conducting an extensive review of the professional literature on this subject, I realized that "exorcism" is often preferred by researchers rather than "deliverance" because of the word's prominent place in historical conversations on this subject. Also, while the words are often used interchangeably, they are not synonymous.

Exorcism is sometimes envisioned as a formal rite used to drive out demons. In other cases, it is applied more generally to any prayers used to expel evil. However, it almost always has the specific focus of combatting diabolic powers, whether real or perceived. My personal application of the term is most closely akin to Psychologist Dennis Bull's definition: "a non-coercive expulsion technique."[2]

By contrast, a broad usage of "deliverance" terminology exists across traditions. While some people use the word to reference casting out demons, others envision it as the fruit of salvation, and still others use it to describe a set of processes employed to lead individuals toward a greater

1. In preparing to write *The Deliverance Dialogues*, I reviewed literature written by pastors, theologians, historians, deliverance ministers, and exorcists from numerous faith traditions, including Pentecostals, Charismatics, Baptists, Lutherans, Methodists, Anglicans, Roman Catholics, and Orthodox churches. I also reviewed publications containing exorcism accounts outside the Christian faith. Among the mental health professionals that are referenced throughout this work, some are Christians and some are not. They are all recognized professionals and leaders in their respective fields. Citation of sources does not represent a full endorsement of the authors or faith traditions. Rather, it is intended to offer a holistic view of the work that is being done to help those who suffer from spiritual or psychological torment.

2. Bull, "A Phenomenological Model," 134.

sense of peace—spirit, soul, and body. Deliverance may include inner healing, counseling, praying the Scriptures, or gaining victory over addictions or compulsions. In everyday conversations and in popular literature, it is applied to a wide array of pastoral practices.

This is not a comprehensive deliverance textbook. It is my humble offering of loaves and fish, placed in the hands of the One who multiplies what is surrendered to him. My prayer is that God will use this work to feed and free multitudes—equipping his people to walk in wisdom, courage, and compassion as they minister in his name. I submit to you, *The Deliverance Dialogues*.

Pastor Robbie Willis, DMin

Acknowledgments

The Deliverance Dialogues OFFERS a fusion of scholarly reflection, pastoral compassion, and critical insights gleaned from boots-on-the-ground deliverance ministry. I am a Pentecostal who deeply values the work that God is doing in the body of Christ at large. As such, this book incorporates research from a variety of faith traditions. It also draws from the contributions of numerous academic disciplines and professions.

Although names and other identifying details from personal stories have been changed for the sake of anonymity, the accounts contained in these pages are real. They tell stories of real pain, real struggles, and of real healing that is found through Jesus Christ. I am grateful to the people who have been brave enough to share their stories, and for the many experts whose research offered vital contributions to this resource.

I would like to express special appreciation to Dr. Carolyn Tennant and Dr. Cory Shipley. Their guidance was of inestimable value throughout the research and writing phase of the project that formed the academic basis for this book at the Assemblies of God Theological Seminary (AGTS). They greatly encouraged me to make this material available to a broader audience. Appreciation also goes out to Dr. Rick Wadholm, who offered guidance with the theological portions of my dissertation, which became chapters 1–4 of this book.

When I reached out to Dr. Siang-Yang Tan to ask if he would consider assessing the chapters that deal with specific mental health conditions, I was unsure if he would respond. He not only returned my message in a timely manner, but he also read the entire manuscript and shared insights and resource recommendations that greatly enriched the quality of this work. Words cannot fully express my appreciation.

Throughout this project, my wife and children have offered tremendous support and encouragement. I am truly grateful for them. My oldest son, Timothy Willis, and I co-host a podcast bearing the same name as this book. Timothy is currently in the final year of a psychology degree. His insights and perspectives have substantially elevated the quality of this work.

Finally, I would like to say thank you to my pastor, David Willis, and to our Link Church family. Pastor David's unceasing support has helped supply the needed space and energy for this project's completion. Link Church is truly a special place, where people from diverse cultural backgrounds gather to worship Jesus Christ in unity. It is a living laboratory, where the truths contained in *The Deliverance Dialogues* are lived out week after week. The blessing that God is pouring out through Link Church is transforming the face of our community, blessing it with strong marriages, healthy families, recovered addicts, and decreased crime and incarceration rates. I am thankful to be part of this journey.

Introduction
From Eternia to Exorcism

I GREW UP WITHOUT cable, before the internet, in a time when TV networks shut down at night and families either cracked open a book or turned off the lights. It was, as my kids would say, *the dark ages*. But there was one shining moment every week—Saturday morning cartoons.

Nothing captured my imagination quite like *He-Man and the Masters of the Universe*. With a bowl of corn flakes in hand, I'd watch Prince Adam raise his sword to the sky and shout, "By the power of Grayskull—I have the power!"[1]

Prince Adam was just an average, awkward guy—much like I was back then. His pet tiger, *Cringer*, lived up to his name. Yet when darkness threatened the land of *Eternia*, Adam tapped into a mysterious power source and became the mighty He-Man.[2] What was this *Grayskull*? Was it simply a fortress—or something symbolic? Looking back, it feels like a relic of a time when we still believed knowledge could save us. Gray matter. Grayskull.[3] In the 1980s, education was king. We were told that smart leaders, strong diplomacy, and growing technology would overcome death, disease, and even nuclear war. Maybe, just maybe, *we* could save Eternia.

Hopes soared as the Berlin Wall fell and the Cold War ended. Yet, even as political walls fell, unseen walls of despair rose. In the decades that followed, terrorism, addiction, mental illness, suicide, abuse, and despair

1. Scheimer, *He-Man*.

2. Scheimer, *He-Man*.

3. I first heard this illustration used to draw a comparison between He-Man and education by Dr. DeLonn Rance during a missions mobilization class that I was taking as part of my master's program at Assemblies of God Theological Seminary. As He-Man was one of my favorite childhood cartoons, it resonated deeply with me.

reminded us that we are still Prince Adam, not He-Man. Knowledge helps, but it cannot save us. The gray matter alone is not enough.

Where was the Church in all this? For many, organized religion seemed part of the problem. As trust in institutions declined, so did faith in spiritual authority. But while churches wrestled with relevance, something unexpected happened: a revival came—but not the kind many expected. In 1990, an estimated 8,000 Americans identified as Wiccan.[4] By 2014, that number had exploded to 1.5 million, surpassing the number of Presbyterians. Paganism surged. Crystals, tarot cards, spirit guides, spells, and spiritual energy became mainstream.[5] We're a "spiritual" society again—just not a Christian one.

At the same time, our nation reached a boiling point of emotional distress. One in five Americans has a diagnosable mental illness.[6] Suicide and addiction devastate families. Medication and therapy help some—but not all. People are searching, desperate for something more. Demons are no longer dismissed—they're trending. Deliverance ministers are booked solid. Exorcists are in demand. People are not asking whether spiritual evil exists; they're asking how to get free.

The Church has a choice. We can scoff and stay silent. Or we can pull up a chair and say, *"Let's talk."* C.S. Lewis warned,

> There are two equal and opposite errors into which our race can fall about the devils. One is to disbelieve in their existence. The other is to believe, and to feel an excessive and unhealthy interest in them. They themselves are equally pleased by both errors and hail a materialist or a magician with the same delight.[7]

This book is about a better way. It is about the *dialogue*—between theology and psychology, between pastors and other professionals, between ancient wisdom and modern insight. It's about deliverance, yes—but also integration, healing, and hope.

Here is the conviction that runs through every chapter: Deliverance is not merely about casting out demons but about holistic cleansing, integration, and discipleship. Pastoral ministry must discern between spiritual oppression and psychological distress while always grounding healing in the person and work of Jesus Christ.

4. Showalter, "Witches Outnumber Presbyterians."
5. Showalter, "Witches Outnumber Presbyterians."
6. NAMI, "Mental Illness by the Numbers."
7. Lewis, *Screwtape Letters*, ix.

This is not a return to superstition or a rejection of science. It's an invitation—a conversation. It is a call to the Church to reclaim its voice in the healing of the soul. This is *The Deliverance Dialogues*.

Chapter 1

When a Shower Won't Fix It

To UNDERSTAND DELIVERANCE FROM spiritual and psychological distress, we need to first look to the pages of Scripture. The Gospel accounts of Christ's exorcism ministry have always intrigued me. As Jesus battled against cosmic forces of darkness, broken humanity found healing. The Bible uses many words to describe what Jesus was waging war against: Satan, demons, evil spirits—but there is one label that is often misunderstood: unclean spirits.[1]

What comes to mind when you hear the word *unclean*? Maybe it's dirt, germs, or something that needs disinfecting. However, in the world of the Bible—especially the Old Testament—*unclean* didn't necessarily mean that you needed a shower because you were "dirty." It meant something far deeper: separation.

To be unclean was to be unfit for the presence of God. It meant exclusion from worship and from the covenant community until restoration came. Uncleanness had to do with anything that symbolized death, disorder, or distance from God's holiness.[2]

In the New Testament, especially in Mark's Gospel, demons are consistently called *unclean spirits*. That's not just a distinction in vocabulary—it's

1. Wright, *Simply Jesus,* 120. Wright asserts, "The battle Jesus was fighting was against the satan. Whatever we think of this theme, it was clearly centrally important for all the gospel writers. . . ."

2. Willis, "Liberation and Integration," chapter 2.

a theological nuance. When the Gospels use the term "unclean spirit," they're telling us something profound about what evil does to people. It separates. It isolates. It defiles. The Bible reveals God's care and concern for humanity as the one who sets distressed individuals free from malicious spiritual powers while simultaneously offering spiritual, mental, and physical healing, integrating those who are liberated into the community of faith.

The Fire That Drew the Line: Nadab, Abihu, and the Language of Clean and Unclean

The language of clean and unclean, holy and common, is not just ancient religious jargon—it is a foundational framework for understanding how God draws lines in the spiritual realm. Before we can rightly discern what is demonic, what is emotional, and what is holy, we need to grasp the biblical vocabulary of distinction. The story of Nadab and Abihu helps us get there.

Though the terms "clean and unclean" appear briefly as early as Genesis 7:2, when God instructed Noah to take pairs of clean and unclean animals into the ark, the concept isn't fully developed until the book of Leviticus—and not coincidentally, right after a tragedy.

> Now Nadab and Abihu, the sons of Aaron, each took his censer and put fire in it and laid incense on it and offered unauthorized fire before the LORD, which He had not commanded them. And fire came out from before the LORD and consumed them, and they died before the LORD (Lev 10:1–2).[3]

Nadab and Abihu were not strangers. They were priests, sons of Aaron himself. They were near to God—literally and vocationally. Yet their nearness came without obedience. They offered incense that was unauthorized, irreverent, unholy—and fire consumed them.

In the aftermath, Moses speaks solemn words to Aaron:

> This is what the LORD has said: "Among those who are near me I will be sanctified, and before all the people I will be glorified." (Lev 10:3)

God was not only calling for worship—He was calling for discernment. And from that moment forward, Yahweh made it clear that those who serve him must learn to distinguish between what is acceptable and what is not.

3. Unless otherwise stated, Bible quotations are taken from the English Standard Version (ESV).

Leviticus 10:10 becomes the divine thesis of this entire priestly handbook:

> You are to distinguish between the holy and the common, and between the unclean and the clean.

This one verse unlocks the rest of the book. Chapters 11–15 unpack how priests are to distinguish between the *unclean and the clean*. Chapters 17–26 explore how to distinguish between the *holy and the common*.[4]

Why does this matter for deliverance? Because spiritual discernment is not just about spotting demons. It's about honoring God's boundaries. Nadab and Abihu died because they blurred the lines. They treated the holy things of God as if they were common—and they brought unauthorized fire into sacred space.

In deliverance ministry, unauthorized fire still destroys. When leaders attempt to cast out spirits without walking in holiness, when people treat spiritual gifts as if they are tools to wield instead of mysteries to steward, the results are dangerous. Confusion enters the room. God is not glorified. The line between what is holy and what is profane gets erased.

God still draws lines. He still calls his people to distinguish between the sacred and the profane, between what is spiritually clean and what is spiritually polluted. He still insists that those who come near him must sanctify him in their approach.

Throughout *The Deliverance Dialogues*, we'll explore these distinctions—because they are not abstract categories. They are spiritual realities that determine whether we walk in life or death, freedom or bondage, light or deception.

What Made People Unclean in the Old Testament?

Leviticus provides the framework: a person could become ritually unclean by touching a dead body, contracting a skin disease, or experiencing certain bodily discharges. None of these things were inherently sinful. Still, they placed a person in a condition that symbolized disorder—something incompatible with the holiness of God.

4. Hartley, *Leviticus*, 139.

"Unclean" was not just about personal hygiene. It was about the presence of death and the loss of wholeness. Uncleanness was a theological diagnosis, not just a physical one.

Now, think about what that meant for real people. To be unclean was to be pushed to the margins of the community. You couldn't enter the temple. You couldn't participate in worship. You were, in a sense, exiled from the presence of God.

But—and this is critical—God made a way back. Sacrifices. Ritual washings. Days of waiting. All these served to restore the unclean person to wholeness and welcome them back into covenant fellowship.

Levitical Law and the Barrier Against the Occult

One of the most overlooked contributions of Leviticus is that its purity laws don't just teach ceremonial cleanliness—they draw a hard line between God's people and the dark spiritual forces of their world.[5] In a culture where occultism was part of everyday life—from fertility cults to necromancy—the holiness code of Leviticus didn't just protect from contamination. It created a barrier against sorcery.

Modern readers sometimes miss this because they view Leviticus as a book of outdated rituals, but scholars like Michael S. Heiser and John Hartley have brought renewed attention to the book's supernatural worldview.[6] In his groundbreaking work *Demons: What the Bible Really Says About the Powers of Darkness*, Heiser notes the deeply spiritual logic behind texts like Leviticus 17:7:

> So they shall no more sacrifice their sacrifices to goat demons,
> after whom they whore.

The wilderness—often a symbol of death and desolation—was historically understood as the dwelling place of evil spirits.[7] Israel's ancient context wasn't neutral. It was a battlefield. The clean/unclean laws, along with the holy/common distinctions, formed the spiritual armor that protected God's people from being lured into idolatry and occult practice.

5. Keener, *Spirit Hermeneutics*, 230–35.

6. Hartley, *Leviticus*, 139; see also, Heiser, *Demons*, 26; see also, Heiser, *The Unseen Realm*, 177. Heiser also notes a "conceptual connection" between the "goat demon" and the scapegoat ritual in Lev 16.

7. Heiser, *Demons*, 26.

Hartley builds on this by showing that even Israel's dietary laws served this function.[8] Animals deemed unclean were often associated with symbols of chaos, confusion, and grotesqueness—features that aligned with sorcerous imagery. He writes:

> Every kind of sorcery is categorically condemned in the laws for holy living (Lev 19:26, 31; 20:6). . . . The regulations governing ritual purity are designed to prevent the practice of sorcery by declaring unclean those animals that symbolize a confusion of classes, ugliness, and desolation—the very symbols loved by wizards and sorcerers.[9]

In other words, Leviticus is not a random assortment of purity codes. It's a strategic safeguard against spiritual defilement, particularly through the occult.

Nowhere is this more evident than in Leviticus 19:26–31, where a sweeping rejection of pagan religious practices is laid out:

> You shall not interpret omens or tell fortunes. . . . You shall not make any cuts on your body for the dead. . . . Do not turn to mediums or necromancers; do not seek them out, and so make yourselves unclean by them: I am the Lord your God.

Heiser explains that English translations tend to dull the intensity of verse 31. His proposed rendering is, "Do not turn to the spirits [*ʾôbôt*], to the ones who have knowledge [*yiddĕʿōnî*]; do not seek them out, and so make yourselves unclean by them: I am Yahweh your God."[10]

The Hebrew terms *ʾôbôt* and *yiddĕʿōnî* appear not only in Leviticus 19 but again in Leviticus 20:6, 27, reinforcing the idea that uncleanness can result from actual engagement with evil spirits, not just from symbolic impurities. While these terms can describe human mediums, Heiser points out that they also refer to the spirits being accessed—which are not neutral forces but demonic entities.[11] He summarizes, "The failure to note that they also refer specifically to supernatural entities results in missing Old Testament terminology for evil spirits."[12]

8. Hartley, *Leviticus*, 145.
9. Hartley, *Leviticus*, 145.
10. Heiser, *Demons*, 17.
11. Heiser, *Demons*, 17–18.
12. Heiser, *Demons*, 17–18.

So, what does this mean for deliverance ministry today? It means we must recover the biblical language of clean and unclean—not as a system of external behaviors, but as a framework for spiritual discernment. Many believers unknowingly blur the lines by dabbling in horoscopes, energy healing, or new age rituals, thinking them harmless. Leviticus reminds us that these things defile, not because of superstition, but because they open doors to real spiritual powers. God's people are called to be holy, and holiness is never passive. It requires us to actively separate from what is unclean, especially when that uncleanness is rooted in darkness.

From Ritual to Spirit: Zechariah's Prophecy and the Rise of the Unclean Spirit

The call to separate from the occult and walk in holiness, as laid out in Leviticus, is not simply about external practices—it's about guarding the people of God from something deeper: a spiritual power that thrives on impurity. This shift from external ritual to internal corruption becomes stunningly clear in the prophecy of Zechariah.

> On that day there shall be a fountain opened for the house of David and the inhabitants of Jerusalem, to cleanse them from sin and uncleanness. . . . And also, I will remove from the land the prophets and the spirit of uncleanness. (Zech 13:1–2)

This passage stands out because it introduces something Leviticus only hinted at: that uncleanness is not just ceremonial—it can be spiritualized and personified. Zechariah is the only Old Testament prophet to refer directly to a "spirit of uncleanness," the very phrase that becomes commonplace in the Gospels, where unclean spirits are cast out again and again by Jesus.[13]

In Leviticus, impurity is mostly addressed at the individual level—bodily emissions, contact with death, dietary violations. But the law also warns of defiling the tabernacle (Lev 15:31) and defiling the camp where God dwells (Num 5:1–3). These warnings become prophetic realities in the

13. Smith, *Micah-Malachi*, 280, Kindle; see also, Jöris, "Markan Use," 50, 59; see also, Baloian, "שָׂטָן (śāṭān), HGK#8477," 1231. While it could be argued that "spirit of uncleanness" here refers simply to a general state of being, Baloian notes, "there is a hint of demonic character in . . . Zech 13:2." Joris writes the following about the term "unclean spirit" on page 59: "[T]he application of the term in Second Temple literature is fairly broad and has connotations of sin and impurity as well as probably denoting a demonic being."

later writings of Ezekiel and Lamentations. God's glory leaves the temple (Ezek 10), and Jerusalem is left desolate because of its impurity (Lam 1:8–10).

By Zechariah's time, the damage has been done. The people have not just flirted with uncleanness—they've embodied it, and the land itself has become saturated with spiritual pollution. Zechariah now speaks of a coming day when a fountain of cleansing will be opened, not just to wash away individual sin, but to remove the unclean spirit from the land entirely.[14]

This is a turning point.

The Hebrew word used here—*niddāh*—is a term loaded with ritual and sexual connotations.[15] It signals a deep kind of defilement, one that cuts people off from both worship and community. And when the ancient Greek translators of the Old Testament rendered *niddāh*, they used words like ἀκαθαρσία, which means impurity or uncleanness—the same word used repeatedly in the New Testament to describe unclean spirits.[16]

Zechariah, then, becomes the interpretive bridge between Leviticus and the Gospels. He links the language of ritual uncleanness to the reality of spiritual corruption, laying the groundwork for Jesus's ministry of casting out unclean spirits. Even more, Zechariah's language prepares the way for a rich understanding of Christ's work on the cross which would at long last bring full and lasting cleansing from the defilement of unclean spirits.

The move from impurity to personified uncleanness is not a theological leap—it's a prophetic progression.

14. While the ESV translates Zechariah's phrase as "the spirit of uncleanness," the NASB and the MEV both translate it as "the unclean spirit." Zechariah 13:2 in the Greek Septuagint uses the same wording that is seen throughout the Gospel of Mark for "unclean spirit."

15. Smith, *Micah-Malachi*, 280; see also, Strong, *Strong's Greek and Hebrew*, h5079, 3131.

16. Averbeck, "דָּוָה (dāwâ), Hebrew GK #1864," 1:928, 1231. This article on *dāwâ* offers insight into *niddah*, Hebrew GK #5614. Here, Richard E. Averbeck notes, "The LXX uses several different G[reek] words to render נִדָּה, the most important being ἄφεδρος, menses (11×; see e.g., Lev 15:19), ῥαντισμός (#4823), sprinkling (6×; Num 19:9, 13, 20, 21 [2×]; Zech 13:1), and ἀκαθαρσία (#174), uncleanness, impurity (4×)." The clear image is that Yahweh's people failed to heed the Levitical warnings and have now been overtaken by ritual impurity. No longer are they simply unclean; there is now a "spirit of uncleanness" that must be removed "from the land" (Zech 13:2).

Why Call a Demon "Unclean"?

Mark's decision to reference "unclean spirits" throughout his gospel instead of "evil spirits" is an editorial decision with deep theological ramifications.[17] To call a demon *unclean* links it directly to the biblical language of impurity and defilement. Identifying demons as unclean spirits suggests that, like uncleanness in the Old Testament, contact with these spirits may bring separation, exclusion, and exile from the people of God. Unclean spirits don't just torment people physically; they disorient the individual's identity and cut them off from spiritual community. Demonization is not just a form of spiritual attack. It introduces spiritual contamination that distorts a person's thinking, emotions, relationships, and sense of self.

Jesus: The Cleanser

In the Gospel of Mark, Jesus emerges as more than a teacher, healer, or even a miracle worker—He is portrayed as the divine cleanser of those rendered unclean by demonic influence. Mark's repeated use of the Greek phrase *pneuma akatharton* ("unclean spirit") carries deep theological significance rooted in the Levitical system of purity and separation. While most readers recognize these spirits as demonic in nature, Mark's language choice intentionally elevates a different dimension of their activity. Rather than using the more general *daimonion* (demon), Mark's preferred terminology underscores the *uncleanness* that results in estrangement from God's covenantal presence and community.

This nuance is vital to Mark's theology of deliverance. As Steffin Joris notes, "it is always a *pneuma akatharton* and never a *daimonion* that speaks in Mark's Gospel."[18] This distinction reveals a deeper Christological intention:

17. Heiser, *Demons*, 197; see also, Kim, "Enochic Traditions," 160; see also, Moscicke, "Gerasene Exorcism," 365. Against Heiser's view that the phrase "unclean spirit" is a reference to the book of First Enoch and is "clear evidence that New Testament writers stood firmly in the Second Temple Jewish tradition regarding the origin of demons," Kim asserts that First Enoch never uses "unclean spirit," but instead Enoch shows a preference for the phrase "evil spirit," which is never used in Mark's Gospel. It appears that Mark was intentionally anchoring his "unclean spirit" language in Leviticus and Zechariah, while perhaps intentionally avoiding Enochian language.

18. Jöris, "Markan Use," 53; see also, Keener, *Miracles*, 2:770–72. On these pages, Keener expounds on the meaning and scope of "*diamones.*" "*Daimonian*" is a Greek word for "demon."

Jesus is not simply casting out demons—He is cleansing defiled people. The use of *pneuma akatharton* recalls the purity codes of Leviticus, where physical and spiritual uncleanness separated people from God's presence, from the tabernacle, and from the community of faith. In this sense, the demonized in Mark are not merely oppressed—they are symbolically cast out from covenant life, unfit for worship, and in need of divine cleansing.

This theological framework connects directly to the prophecy in Zechariah 13. There, Yahweh promises to open "a fountain. . .to cleanse them from sin and uncleanness" (v. 1) and to "remove. . . the spirit of uncleanness from the land" (v. 2).[19] Mark views Jesus's ministry as the fulfillment of this prophecy.[20]

Understanding exorcism through this lens reorients our interpretation of Jesus's miracles. His authority over unclean spirits is not simply an act of spiritual warfare; it is an act of covenant restoration. As Kim affirms, "Since being rendered clean allows one to participate in the worship of the community again . . . Mark very likely says that Jesus's exorcism was a way of restoring people in God's chosen community."[21]

This reading of Mark's exorcism accounts paints Jesus not merely as a miracle worker or healer of the disturbed, but as the divine priest who enacts the long-awaited purification foretold by the prophets. He fulfills the Levitical codes by cleansing what the law could only diagnose. He does what the sacrificial system pointed toward but could never complete. His exorcisms are eschatological acts—signs that the Kingdom of God has come and that the age of cleansing and restoration has begun.[22]

In short, Jesus's ministry of deliverance is not peripheral to the Gospel—it is central. He is the One who purifies, restores, and reclaims what has been defiled. Through him, the exiled are brought home, the unclean are made whole, and the tormented find peace. He is not just another exorcist. He is the *fountain* opened for all who long to be clean.

19. Silva, "καθαρός," 571; see also, Strong, *Strong's Greek and Hebrew*, h7307, 3791 and h2932, 2497. The Hebrew phrase used in Zech 13:2 is "*ruwach tu'mah*." In the LXX, this is translated as "*pneuma akathartos*," which is the Synoptic phrase for "unclean spirit." Other Hebrew words closely related to "*tu'mah*" and often translated "unclean" are h2930, "*tame*'" and h2931, "*tame*'." The portion that is quoted in the main text above is from a subsection within the cited text from Silva in which "*akathartos*" is shown to be the opposite of "καθαρός".

20. Kim, "Enochic Traditions," 160; see also, Willis, "Liberation and Integration," 39. Kim cites several factors that support this connection.

21. Kim, "Enochic Traditions," 158.

22. Moscicke, "Gerasene Exorcism," 363–83.

Uncleanness and the Church Today

We have people in our communities and churches today who feel unclean. They may not have a skin disease or live among tombs, but they carry shame, trauma, addiction, or torment. Like the demoniac that we will discuss at length in chapter 2, many live in self-imposed exile, believing they are beyond hope.

Some of them are spiritually oppressed. Others are emotionally shattered. Some are mentally ill. Some may be all of the above. That's why the church must rediscover what Jesus understood: deliverance is not just a dramatic confrontation—it's a ministry of cleansing. When we minister to the oppressed, we are offering more than emotional support. We are opening the gates to holiness, community, and restoration.

Micah's Story: The Cry Behind the Chaos

Micah grew up in a Christian home. There was nothing particularly troubling about his childhood—no open rebellion and no obvious red flags. His mother was a devoted homemaker, deeply involved in his life. His father, though loving, was often preoccupied with work, illness, and a cascade of personal responsibilities. Micah never voiced resentment. He just grew quieter.

It was during his early teenage years that things began to unravel. Micah and his sister both came down with a stomach virus. While she recovered quickly, Micah's symptoms lingered. He lost weight rapidly. Weeks turned into months, and after multiple doctor visits and even an overnight hospital stay, no clear diagnosis emerged.

His mother started to suspect something deeper. Micah was still insisting that he was sick, but she began to wonder if he was pretending. Was this an eating disorder? Was it some other kind of psychological struggle?

One afternoon, she confronted him. The response was immediate and disturbing. Micah erupted in rage. His father, already on edge from life's pressures, was called home immediately. As he stepped through the door, he found his son lying in a puddle of vomit, limp and silent on the floor. Whatever he had expected, it wasn't this. Nonetheless, it became a clarifying moment: the illness, the denial, the anger—it all pointed to something far more serious.

They pressed him for answers. Micah shouted. Then, in an instant, his expression changed. Terror filled his eyes, the kind of terror reserved for someone who had just witnessed something unspeakable. He cried out, "Help me! The voices won't stop. I need you to help me!"

Micah collapsed to the floor, screaming, his body twisting into unnatural positions. His eyes rolled back. He became unresponsive—unable to speak, unable to hear. The atmosphere in the house shifted. It no longer felt like a domestic crisis. It felt like a spiritual ambush.

His parents, overwhelmed and desperate, began calling on the name of Jesus. A family friend joined them, commanding any unclean spirit to release its grip. It was not rehearsed. It was not polished. It was raw, urgent intercession.

In that moment, the presence of God filled the room and there was peace. Micah's body stilled. His eyes cleared. His voice returned. The chaos lifted like fog burned away by the morning sun, but the story didn't end with that moment.

In the days that followed, something in Micah softened. He began initiating hugs—something he had rarely done before. He leaned his head on his parents' shoulders. For the first time, he started talking—really talking—about what had been going on inside him.

He spoke about struggles with food, rooted in offhand comments about his weight that had quietly bruised his identity. He spoke about feeling invisible, like his dad had time for everyone except him. He confessed to long-standing fear and anxiety—how he would sometimes see shadows, hear whispers, and constantly feel afraid.

The deliverance had opened the door, but the healing. . .that would take time. There were hard conversations. His father had to face his own regrets. Micah had to learn how to trust again. They both had to rebuild a relationship from the inside out. Although Micah was free from the torment that had overtaken him that day, he still had a journey ahead before fully surrendering his life to Jesus.

His healing was not linear. It involved doctors who ruled out medical causes. There were counselors who helped him sort through anxiety and pastors who prayed and discipled him. Family members pulled closer to him, and friends offered companionship. These people all made a huge difference in his life, but still, the spiritual war had to be confronted head-on.

Micah's story reminds us that uncleanness, as Scripture presents it, is not just a metaphor for sin. It's a spiritual condition that can take root in the soul, distorting truth and suffocating joy. When it manifests—sometimes violently—our only hope is in the cleansing power of Jesus Christ. Micah's breakthrough did not come through shouting or formulas. It came through love, truth, and the persistent light of Christ piercing the darkness.

A Theology of Cleansing

Christ cleanses the unclean and welcomes them into his family. The voice of Jesus rises above the noise of the enemy, saying: *You are not what tormented you. You are not what touched you. You are mine, and I make you whole.*

Uncleanness is not primarily about sin. Rather, it is about exclusion from God's people and presence. Demons, then, are described as unclean spirits because they are spiritually toxic; they isolate, distort, dehumanize, and desecrate.

That's the kind of clarity that is needed today. Demons aren't just scary. They are corrupting. Jesus didn't just come to expel them—He came to cleanse the temple, and that includes the temple of the human heart.

In the next chapter, we will discuss a man so tormented that he lived among the tombs. You may not see yourself in him, but maybe you know someone who lives isolated in shame. On the other hand, maybe you're battling a sense of fear, rejection, or torment that feels like it defines you.

Here's the good news: what Jesus did then, he still does now. He cleanses the unclean. He welcomes the excluded. He reclaims what darkness tried to destroy, and he's still the fountain opened for us today.

Questions to Discuss

Take time to write down your answers to the questions at the end of each chapter and discuss them with another individual or with a group.

1. How does the biblical definition of "unclean" challenge our modern assumptions about sin, shame, and separation from God?
2. In what ways can "blurring the lines" between the holy and the common, as Nadab and Abihu did, still happen in today's church or ministry settings?
3. What are some subtle ways believers today might open the door to spiritual uncleanness without realizing it?
4. How does Mark's emphasis on "unclean spirits" (instead of simply "demons") deepen our understanding of deliverance as covenant restoration?

Chapter 2

The Clash of Kingdoms

Jesus did not invent the concept of demonization, nor was he the first figure in Jewish history to confront unclean spirits. Yet, his ministry of liberation reverberated with an authority that shook the spiritual foundations of the ancient world. When he freed a man in the synagogue from demonic torment, the onlookers were stunned. "What is this? A new teaching with authority! He commands even the unclean spirits, and they obey him" (Mark 1:27b). The astonishment was not that exorcism had occurred, but that it had happened through a word—calm, unritualized, and unmistakably effective.[1] Jesus was not the kind of exorcist they were used to. His "new teaching" was not a technique but a revelation—one that set captives free and restored peace in places once held in bondage. What made his teaching new was not novelty, but power.

One of the most gripping scenes in all of Scripture unfolds on the eastern shore of the Sea of Galilee. A man, naked and tormented, roams among the tombs. He cries out night and day, cutting himself with stones.

1. Whiston, *Works of Josephus*, Ant. 8:2.5. The first century historian, Josephus, describes the actions of a Jewish exorcist in the presence of the emperor, Vespasian. His account offers a window into how exorcism was approached by others in that era. The exorcist "put a ring that had a root of one of those sorts mentioned by Solomon to the nostrils of the demoniac; after which he drew out the demon through his nostrils, and when the man fell down, he adjured him to return no more." It is not difficult to see what was different about Christ's approach.

The townspeople have tried everything—chains, shackles, isolation—but nothing could restrain him. . .nothing, that is, until Jesus steps ashore.

The Gospel of Mark gives us the most detailed account of this encounter (Mark 5:1–20). It's not just a story of a man delivered from demonic oppression—it's a cosmic showdown. This moment reveals the power of Christ's kingdom over the darkness that torments humanity. It is the clearest image in the Gospels of what it looks like when Jesus confronts the full fury of demonic power.

Suffering Under Spiritual Siege: Jewish Views of Demonic Affliction in the Second Temple Era

The intense suffering of the demonized man in the Gospels—a man isolated from society, tormented in body and mind, and driven to self-destruction—is not foreign to the biblical imagination. In fact, it fits well within the worldview held by many in Second Temple Judaism, the cultural and religious backdrop of Jesus's earthly ministry. For these first-century Jews, demons were not theoretical—they were tangible, personal, and terrifying.

One such glimpse into this worldview is found in the apocryphal book of Tobit. There, we meet a woman named Sarah, who is haunted by the demon Asmodeus.[2] This spirit kills seven men who marry her—each before the marriage can be consummated. Her story is one of grief and confusion. No one around her understands what is happening. Eventually, she is so distraught that she contemplates suicide, crying out to God to end her life.[3] Her pain is not presented as a moral failure—but as the anguish of someone trapped in spiritual bondage.

This theme of demonization as torment continues in 1 Enoch, particularly in the *Book of the Watchers*. This influential Jewish text describes evil spirits as agents of suffering. These spirits are said to:

> Afflict, oppress, destroy, attack, do battle, and work destruction on the earth, and cause trouble. . . .[4]

2. Neubauer, *Book of Tobit*, Tobit Ch. 3. Tobit was written in the second or third century BCE.

3. Neubauer, *Tobit*, Ch. 3.

4. 1 Enoch 15:10–11. All references to 1 Enoch are from Schneiders, *Complete edition*.

They aren't simply symbols of internal struggle—they are supernatural forces of chaos. These writings, while not considered Scripture, help us understand how the average Jewish person of Jesus's time viewed demonic activity: it was personal, powerful, and invasive.

The *Book of Jubilees*, written by a Pharisaic Jew in the second century BCE, builds upon the ideas found in Enoch. In its retelling of the Torah story, Jubilees introduces a demonic hierarchy under the authority of a Satan-like figure named Mastema.[5] Though human beings are still held accountable for their actions, the text acknowledges that:

> Malignant spirits assisted and seduced them into committing transgression and uncleanness.[6]

These spirits are not merely whisperers of temptation. They are agents of corruption and destruction, sowing bloodshed and spiritual impurity across the earth.[7]

This spiritual worldview—deeply rooted in apocalyptic literature—was part of the collective consciousness of the Jewish people when Jesus began his public ministry. The Gospels do not begin with philosophical debates about the origin of evil; they begin with Jesus confronting it head-on. In that confrontation, he doesn't pause to explain the metaphysics of Mastema or the lineage of Asmodeus. He does something more powerful—He casts the spirits out.

Jesus does not validate every tradition from the intertestamental writings, but he doesn't reject their underlying concern either. He enters a world where demons are real, suffering is spiritual, and people are held in invisible chains—and he brings liberation.

The Jewish literature of the Second Temple period reminds us that suffering from demonic oppression is not a modern invention, nor is it exclusive to pagan cultures. It was a known reality to the very people Jesus came to save. While their writings don't hold the same authority as Scripture, they help us appreciate the gravity of the spiritual warfare Jesus walked into—and the profound relief that came when he spoke a word of deliverance.

5. *Jubilees 10:8–9*. All references to *Jubilees* are from Charles, *Book of Jubilees*.

6. *Jubilees*, 11:3.

7. *Jubilees*, 11:4.

A Man Possessed, a Region Oppressed

The man possessed by Legion is introduced as "a man with an unclean spirit." That phrase matters. It tells us right away that this is about more than mental illness, more than trauma, more than sin. This man is under the influence of a spiritual presence that has defiled and desecrated him from the inside out.

A profound detail in Mark's account is the way Jesus distinguishes between the man and the spirit tormenting him. Before describing his maniacal condition, Mark identifies him simply as "a man" (Mark 5:2). Though he lives among the tombs, breaks chains with supernatural strength, and cries out in agony day and night, his humanity is not erased by his affliction. Jesus affirms this distinction when he issues the command, "Come out of the man, you unclean spirit" (v. 8). The demonic identity is named and confronted, but the man himself is never confused with the evil that inhabits him.

This separation is crucial—not only in the narrative but for every pastor or counselor engaged in deliverance today. People are not demons. Their dignity, however marred, remains intact. To conflate the person with the spirit is to risk dehumanizing the very one Christ came to restore. Deliverance begins with this foundational recognition: beneath every manifestation is a soul loved by God.

The demonized man is a symbol of utter devastation. He lives among the dead, isolated from family and community. His body bears the scars of self-harm. His soul is fractured, his mind consumed. He's the living embodiment of exile.

When Jesus steps onto the shore, this man runs—not away, but toward him. The text says he ran and *worshiped* him. The spirits within him recognized who Jesus was, but there's something deeper happening: this tormented man, somewhere deep in his buried will, recognizes the One who can restore him.

Naming the Enemy: "My Name Is Legion"

Jesus asks the spirit's name. The answer is chilling: "My name is Legion, for we are many." This wasn't just one spirit—this man was overrun by an army. The use of Roman military language isn't accidental.[8] This is warfare.

8. Vaughan, *Phenomenal Phenomena*, 148. "Legion" is a Latin military term referring to a group of about 5,600 Roman soldiers.

It's a battle not only for a man's soul but also for the region he inhabits. The spirits beg Jesus not to send them out of the territory (Mark 5:10), perhaps revealing their desire to hold dominion over that land.

Here, we're reminded that demons don't just seek to inhabit individuals—they aim to influence territories, cultures, families, and systems. Deliverance is not only about personal freedom. It's about breaking the grip of darkness on entire communities.

Unclean Spirits and Unclean Places

The story of the Gerasene demoniac is steeped in the language and imagery of Levitical uncleanness. The man lives "among the tombs" (Mark 5:1, 5), placing him in constant contact with the dead—an act that, according to Numbers 19, renders a person ceremonially unclean (Num 19:11–22). Like the leper described in Leviticus, he is "always crying out" (Mark 5:5; cf. Lev 13:45) and lacks appropriate clothing, a detail that Luke highlights by stating he "had not worn clothes for a long time" (Luke 8:27). Every feature of the man's condition—his isolation, exposure, torment, and uncleanness—points to a life utterly defiled. The unclean pigs, the Gentile setting, and the man's tormented existence present a vivid portrait of impurity at every level: personal, cultural, and spiritual. The setting itself cries out for cleansing, and into this spiritual wasteland steps Jesus, the Holy One, with power to purify both the man and the land.

The spirits beg to be sent into a herd of pigs. In that moment, the uncleanness that had corrupted the man is transferred to another unclean vessel. This is a reversal of everything the enemy tried to do. The man, once among the tombs, is now restored. The spirits, once hidden within a person, are now exposed and expelled. Jesus demonstrates that his authority is not just spiritual—it's total. He commands unclean spirits, and they obey. He speaks, and the powers of death flee.

If this man is indeed a Gentile, then he is not beholden to Israel's clean and unclean laws—but that only intensifies the force of Mark's Levitical language. The imagery is intentional. The defilement of the man, the pigs, and the region paints a picture of impurity that transcends covenant boundaries, and yet, Christ crosses those boundaries. He walks into Gentile territory, confronts the unclean spirits, and makes the man whole.

In this moment, the fountain promised in Zechariah 13:1 is opened not only for Israel, but for the nations. The cleansing power of Christ flows beyond Jerusalem's temple and saturates even the most unclean places. Jesus does not just liberate one man—He announces that his kingdom brings purity, peace, and restoration to all who are defiled, Jew and Gentile alike.

The Tenth Roman Legion

Recent historical and archaeological evidence shows that Gerasa, part of the Decapolis, served as a regional Roman stronghold during the early to mid-first century.[9] Roman coins and inscriptions from this area feature the symbol of the wild boar, representing *Legio X Fretensis*, a Roman legion stationed in the region.[10] The boar was a military emblem, a proud declaration of Rome's strength.

Perhaps what Jesus does here is more than merely a spiritual deliverance. Rather, it appears to be a prophetic act of defiance. The unclean spirits identifying as "Legion" are expelled into pigs—symbolic of Rome's occupying forces—and then hurled into the sea, a biblical image of chaos and judgment. This isn't just a healing story; it's a kingdom clash.

In this single moment, Jesus makes it clear: the kingdom of God is greater than Rome, and he—*not Caesar*—is King.[11]

The death of the pigs is more than collateral damage. It is a cosmic protest, a visible sign that the powers which enslave and destroy—whether demonic or imperial—are subject to the authority of Jesus Christ. In a region marked by Roman presence, imperial propaganda, and spiritual darkness, the drowning of the swine announces that a new order has come.[12] In case there's any doubt about what this means for people: the man who had been tormented is soon sitting clothed and in his right mind—a living testimony to the healing power of Jesus over both spiritual and systemic oppression.

Restoration: Clothed and in His Right Mind

What happens next is one of the most beautiful scenes in the entire Gospel story. When the townspeople come to see what has happened, they find the man *"sitting there, clothed and in his right mind."* This is more than a

9. Hogeterp, "Trauma and Its Ancient Literary Representation," 11.

10. Hogeterp, "Trauma and Its Ancient Literary Representation," 19.

11. This is especially significant since tradition handed down by Papias holds that Mark wrote his Gospel based on sermons Peter preached in Rome.

12. Garroway, "Invasion of a Mustard Seed," 59–60.

return to sanity. It's a picture of full integration. The man who had been fragmented, tormented, and naked is now whole, peaceful, and dressed in dignity. Here's what I find most powerful: Jesus doesn't just deliver him—He commissions him.

When the man begs to follow Jesus, the Lord tells him to go home and tell his people "what the Lord has done for you and how he had mercy on you." (Mark 5:19) Deliverance leads to discipleship. Restoration leads to mission. He becomes the first evangelist to the Decapolis—ten cities known for their idolatry and paganism. He is no longer a prisoner of darkness; he's a witness to the light.

Deliverance Is Not a Spectacle—It's a Sign

This passage teaches us that deliverance is not entertainment. It's not performance. It is a holy confrontation between the kingdom of God and the kingdom of darkness.

What Jesus does for this man, he still does for people today, for those who are tormented, isolated, and cut off. He still offers hope to those living among the tombs—sometimes literal, sometimes emotional, sometimes spiritual. Jesus still crosses seas to rescue them. This man was not just freed from something. He was freed *for* something—for purpose, for community, and for testimony.

What about the townspeople? They were afraid. They asked Jesus to leave. The power they witnessed was too great, too disruptive, too holy for their comfort. That's still true today—sometimes deliverance scares religious systems more than the oppression ever did. Jesus came to confront what others tolerate.

The Clash Still Happens

This story reminds us that spiritual warfare isn't metaphorical. There are real powers at work in the world that aim to isolate, torment, and destroy. Thankfully, there is also a real King—Jesus—who steps into our brokenness with authority and compassion.

Deliverance is not always immediate, and it's not always loud, but it is always possible in the presence of Jesus. The man who was once bound became a missionary. The region that once trembled became a testimony. That is the power of the gospel.

Zoe's Story

The spiritual conflict of Mark 5 is echoed in unsettling, yet redemptive ways in the life of a young woman named Zoe. By the age of seven, Zoe had spent nearly half her life bouncing among various foster placements. Her behavior was explosive—violent, profane, and unmanageable. She attended a special school that was usually reserved for troubled teens requiring isolation and had been in and out of behavioral health hospitals for her entire life. Some specialists labeled her condition as Reactive Attachment Disorder (RAD); others said it was Post-Traumatic Stress Disorder (PTSD) paired with severe Attention Deficit Hyperactivity Disorder (ADHD) and Oppositional Defiant Disorder (ODD). Medication failed. Therapy yielded no breakthrough. One professional described her as a wounded creature, "like a caged animal—angry and terrified." The more people tried to love her, the more violently she pushed them away.

Her past was a mosaic of tragedy: abuse, neglect, exposure to substances, and abandonment. No single trauma could fully account for her pain—it was the weight of it all. She seemed irreparably broken, but just as Jesus once stepped onto the shores of Gerasa, he walked into Zoe's story. Her new foster parents were devoted but exhausted. At times, they had to restrain her for hours just to keep her from inflicting harm. One afternoon, as chaos erupted once again, her foster father desperately cried out to God for help. That's when something unexpected happened.

Their preteen son entered the room with tears running down his cheeks. Looking at his sister with grief and compassion, he cried out, "In the Name of Jesus Christ, come out of her and stop doing this to her!" What happened next can only be described by one word: *peace*. The storm that raged in Zoe suddenly stilled. The house fell quiet. The torment ceased.

This was not the end of Zoe's journey, but it was the moment everything changed. Over the following months, under careful supervision, her medical team began tapering her off all medications. Therapy, which had previously been ineffective, began producing real results. Her mind cleared. Her heart softened. She went to church, became able to stay in the classroom at school, had playdates with friends, and slowly began to heal.

Eventually, her foster family adopted her. Today, Zoe is thriving. She still has hard days. The pain of the past does not vanish overnight. Still, what began as a dramatic deliverance unfolded into a long, beautiful process of integrative healing. Jesus restored her dignity, reclaimed her identity, and gave her a future. Like the man in the tombs, Zoe was once bound and tormented, but she is now clothed, restored, and sitting at peace. The same Jesus who calmed the storm in Gerasa continues to bring freedom today—to individuals, families, and even regions, one life at a time.

Questions to Discuss

1. In what ways did Jesus's deliverance of the man with the legion differ from the exorcism traditions of his time, and why is his "calm authority" so significant for ministry today?
2. The text highlights how Jesus separates the man's identity from the spirit tormenting him. Why is this distinction vital in pastoral care and deliverance, and what can happen when we fail to make it?
3. Why do you think the townspeople asked Jesus to leave after witnessing the deliverance, and how might fear of disruption keep people from embracing freedom today?
4. Zoe's story mirrors the man in Mark 5 in many ways. What does her journey teach us about the relationship between dramatic deliverance and the ongoing process of healing and discipleship?

Chapter 3

The Key to Sustained Freedom

When Jesus delivered the demonized, he did more than silence spirits—He restored shattered souls. Deliverance is powerful, but it is not the end of the journey. It is the beginning of something sacred: the process of sanctification.

Sanctification means to be set apart—separated from sin and unto God. It is a divine act and an ongoing process. It is essential, because unclean spirits are not merely cast out; they must be replaced by something greater. If they aren't, they may return.

In Luke 11, Jesus tells a sobering parable:

> When the unclean spirit has gone out of a person, it passes through waterless places seeking rest, and finding none it says, 'I will return to my house from which I came.' And when it comes, it finds the house swept and put in order. Then it goes and brings seven other spirits more evil than itself, and they enter and dwell there, and the last state of that person is worse than the first. (Luke 11:24–26)

This is why sanctification matters. Freedom must be followed by formation. Deliverance must be accompanied by discipleship.[1] Jesus doesn't just clean the house—He takes up residence in it.

1. Chiang, *Importance of Inner Healing*, 57–77. Chiang, an Assemblies of God scholar, demonstrates that there is an inseparable relationship between inner healing and deliverance, sanctification, and discipleship. On pages 74–77, he argues that inner

Scripture teaches us that sanctification comes through three primary channels: the Blood, the Spirit, and the Truth. Each plays a vital role in ensuring that deliverance is not only received but retained. Let's explore them more closely.

Sanctification by the Blood

Jesus spoke plainly in Mark 7 about what truly defiles a person. Contrary to ritualistic traditions, defilement doesn't come from external things. It comes from within:

> What comes out of a person is what defiles him. For from within, out of the heart of man, come evil thoughts, sexual immorality, theft, murder, adultery . . . All these evil things come from within, and they defile a person. (Mark 7:20–23)

Defilement makes people vulnerable to unclean spirits. But the solution to inward uncleanness is not stricter rules—it's the blood of Jesus.

> On that day there shall be a fountain opened for the house of David and the inhabitants of Jerusalem, to cleanse them from sin and uncleanness. (Zech 13:1)

The blood of Jesus is that fountain.

Hebrews affirms that:

> By one offering he has perfected forever those who are being sanctified. (Heb 10:14)

And again:

> We have been sanctified through the offering of the body of Jesus Christ once for all. (Heb 10:10)

The cross is not just about forgiveness; it's about transformation. The same blood that secures our justification also works to sanctify us. Wolfgang Vondey captures the experience in powerful terms:

> Sanctification as a tarrying practice contains the confession of sin and the surrender of one's sinful nature to God. . . as a physical and sometimes violent struggle of the flesh. . . . Believers tarry for

healing and deliverance represent an opportunity for individuals to experience Christ's sanctification in a participatory manner as opposed to merely imitating him through progressively improved morality.

> Jesus, both in an active separation from the world, and through participation in the sanctifying presence of Christ. There is no Pentecostal tarrying without Jesus, since believers are sanctified by his blood (1 John 1:7; Heb 10:10; Rev 1:5).[2]

Deliverance isn't clean and clinical. It's often messy, vulnerable, and embodied, but the blood of Jesus is enough.

When someone is sanctified by the blood, the chains that gave unclean spirits access are broken. Not just the spirit's presence—but the conditions of its habitation—are confronted.

Sanctification by the Spirit

The Spirit of God is not only the power behind deliverance—He is also the person who sanctifies the believer. Paul writes:

> that the offering of the Gentiles may be acceptable, sanctified by the Holy Spirit. (Rom 15:16)

This sanctifying work is not abstract. It is demonstrated in power, signs, and wonders (v. 19). The Holy Spirit purifies by fire and leads people into obedience.

In 1 Corinthians 6, Paul lists numerous defiling sins—exactly the kind of sins that leave people open to the enemy. But then he offers hope:

> And such were some of you. But you were washed, you were sanctified, you were justified. . . by the Spirit of our God. (1 Cor 6:11)

Vondey writes:

> The Pentecostal experience of the Lord is accompanied by the witness of the Holy Spirit in physical manifestations that can range from the inward sense of deliverance from sin to the dramatic exorcism of a demonic spirit. Christians are sanctified by the Holy Spirit (Rom 15:16; 1 Cor 6:11; 1 Pet 1:2).[3]

The Holy Spirit does not just empower ministry. He enacts holiness.

Where the Spirit is, there is freedom (2 Cor. 3:17)—freedom from the grip of sin, freedom from torment, freedom to walk in joy. He also leads us into discipline, accountability, and fellowship. Sanctification by the Spirit

2. Vondey, *Pentecostal Theology*, 64.
3. Vondey, *Pentecostal Theology*, 64.

is both encounter and transformation. He drives out demons and then rebuilds character.

Sanctification by the Truth

The Gospel of John contains no exorcism narratives. This isn't an oversight—it's a theological statement. "Satan is not confronted in the form of sickness caused by demons," writes Graham Twelftree, "but in the form of unbelief inspired by the father of lies. So exorcism is not the response to demon possession; truth is its antidote."[4]

Jesus confronts Satan not by spectacle—but with truth. He tells the Pharisees:

> You are of your father the devil. . . . He was a murderer from the beginning . . . there is no truth in him. (John 8:44)

And to those who would listen, Jesus offers a path to freedom:

> If you abide in my word, you are truly my disciples, and you will know the truth, and the truth will set you free. (John 8:31–32)

Truth has an exorcistic function. Lies give demons access; truth exposes them and drives them out.

Jesus prays for his disciples:

> Sanctify them in the truth; your word is truth. (John 17:17)

Paul builds on this in Ephesians 4. Those who are separated from God are:

> Darkened in their understanding. . . . (v. 18)

But those who follow Christ are:

> Renewed in the spirit of your minds. . . . (v. 23)[5]

The result? They put away falsehood (v. 25), guard their anger (v. 26), and give no opportunity to the devil (v. 27).

Sanctification by the truth reshapes thinking and reforms behavior. It renews the mind, heals the memory, and cuts off the lies that demons feed on.

4. Twelftree, *In the Name of Jesus*, 282. Twelftree's reflection is here focused on John's Gospel.

5. Silva, "νοῦς, G5706," 431. Silva notes, "The mind is also the locus of spiritual struggle: as the true inner self that distinguishes between good and bad."

Valerie's Story: The Power of Forgiveness and the Sanctifying Truth

I witnessed the liberating power of truth first-hand during a series of revival services at a local church. When a young teenager named Valerie was brought forward for prayer, a staff member explained that she demonstrated signs of deep torment. They described how Valerie spoke in different voices throughout the night while sleeping, and how her distress had only worsened with prayer.

As we prayed, I sensed a demonic presence. There were physical manifestations—brief, intense moments of resistance—but then, suddenly, peace. Valerie appeared free. My wife and I left that church rejoicing in what God had done.

When we returned the following year, however, the pastors pulled me aside with a grim update. "There's a young woman in the church causing all kinds of disruption—severe torment, worse than ever before." As they spoke, I realized with sinking clarity that they were talking about Valerie.

"Pastor," I said, "God set her free last year." He looked at me and said words I'll never forget: "Robbie, she's worse than she's ever been."

Devastated, my wife and I returned to our room and cried out to God for direction. That night, Valerie came forward again. Once more, demonic manifestations appeared, followed by apparent relief. Tragically, by the next night, things had escalated beyond what we could have imagined. She was crawling on all fours, licking car bumpers in the parking lot, and acting like an animal. The scene was heartbreaking. I remembered Jesus's warning in Matthew 12, that when an unclean spirit leaves a person and finds no rest, it may return with seven spirits more wicked than itself. I wasn't sure what we were missing—but it was clear that exorcism alone wasn't enough. Something deeper was needed.

We continued seeking God for guidance. The next to last night of the revival, Valerie came forward yet again. This time, however, I didn't rush to her side. Instead, I stood back as my wife, Anna May, and others gathered around her to pray. What happened next revealed a truth we had not yet fully understood: Deliverance requires sanctifying grace, and sanctification requires truth.

One of the intercessors sensed that Valerie was harboring unforgiveness. As they explored this, she flippantly listed names as if she were playing a game. That was when the Holy Spirit spoke to Anna May; Valerie needed to forgive her father. When Anna May gently mentioned it, Valerie's entire demeanor shifted. Something had been exposed. Anna May explained that forgiveness doesn't absolve someone of their responsibility before God, but it does release the offense from the hands of the wounded. Bitterness, she explained, was exacting a devastating toll on Valerie's soul.

At first, Valerie just whispered the words, "I forgive my dad." She said them again. Then again. On the seventh time, she broke. With tears streaming down her face, she cried out, "I forgive him. I do. I forgive him."

At that moment, my wife embraced her and prayed. There were no screams, no shaking, no violent manifestations. Just peace. Just freedom.

The next night, Valerie returned with a bag full of items and asked if we could burn it. I never looked inside. I didn't need to. Whatever those things were, they no longer had a hold on her. When we returned to that church a year later, Valerie was radiant. Her mind was clear, her spirit was free, and she was still on fire for Jesus.

Valerie's healing came not just through the command of deliverance, but through the power of sanctification—through the blood of Jesus, the ministry of the Holy Spirit, and, critically, the sanctifying truth that set her free. Truth breaks the lies of bitterness. Truth silences the torment. Truth exorcises demons.

Forgiveness and the Tormentors: An Exposition of Matthew 18: 21—35

Valerie's story begs the question: what's the big deal about unforgiveness? Matthew chapter 18 offers an answer. Here, Peter approaches Jesus with a sincere—and relatable—question: "Lord, how often shall my brother sin against me, and I forgive him? Up to seven times?" (v. 21). Jesus responds not with a number, but with a principle: "I do not say to you up to seven times, but up to seventy times seven" (v. 22, MEV). Then, to drive the point home, he tells a parable that paints a vivid—and sobering—picture of the power of forgiveness.

A king begins settling accounts with his servants and comes to one who owes him an astronomical sum: ten thousand talents. In the time of Christ, one talent was the equivalent of about twenty years' wages for a common laborer. That means this servant owed the equivalent of two hundred thousand years of labor—roughly two thousand lifetimes of debt. There was no realistic way for this debt to ever be repaid.

When the servant begs for patience and mercy, the king astonishingly cancels the entire debt. It's a moment of unimaginable grace. This scene is a beautiful picture of salvation—God's mercy toward us in Christ.

But Jesus doesn't end the story there.

No sooner is the man forgiven than he finds a fellow servant who owes him a hundred denarii—about a hundred days' wages. Compared to what he had just been forgiven, it's a pittance. Still, he seizes the man, demands repayment, and when the man begs for mercy, he refuses. He has him thrown into debtor's prison.

When the other servants witness this hypocrisy, they report it to the king. Enraged, the king confronts the forgiven servant: "Should you not also have had mercy on your fellow servant, just as I had mercy on you?" (v. 33). In his fury, he hands him over to the jailers—what the King James Version calls the "tormentors"—until the debt is paid.

Then Jesus lands the blow:

> So my heavenly Father also will do to each of you, if from his heart he does not forgive his brother his trespasses." (v. 35)

This parable reveals a spiritual law: *forgiveness received must become forgiveness given.* If we hold on to offense, bitterness, or resentment—even after receiving God's grace—we place ourselves in spiritual captivity. The torment Jesus speaks of is real. Sometimes it manifests emotionally, sometimes mentally, and sometimes physically. But it always leads to bondage.

Unforgiveness is a prison—but it's one with the key on the inside.[6]

This teaching is essential to deliverance ministry. Many people remain tormented not because they haven't received forgiveness, but because they haven't extended it. Demonic oppression often finds legal ground in bitterness. Freedom, then, requires more than confession; it requires release. The decision to forgive, even when it's hard, breaks chains that the enemy depends on. Jesus didn't just come to cancel debts. He came to teach us how to live free, and freedom requires forgiveness.

The Fullness of Sanctifying Grace

Deliverance is amazing, but it's not enough unless it's followed by sanctification. People must be cleansed, filled, and formed. As Vondey explains:

6. Lewis, *Problem of Pain*, 112. Lewis wrote, "I willingly believe that the damned are, in one sense, successful rebels to the end; that the doors of hell are locked on the inside."

> The fullness—not a portion—of sanctifying grace is poured out by the Holy Spirit. . . Deliverance and being set free. . . refer to a concrete and repeated sense of liberation from sin, addiction, sickness, and even demon-possession.[7]

The house must be swept clean; yes, but it must also be filled with light.

In the New Testament, sanctification comes through the blood of Jesus, the power of the Spirit, and the liberating truth of God's Word. Deliverance is the doorway, but sanctification is the journey.

The Spirit of Truth and the Process of Change

Jesus referred to the Holy Spirit as the "Spirit of truth" (John 16:13). That title isn't just poetic—it's strategic. The enemy traffics in lies, accusations, and illusions, but the Spirit brings clarity, conviction, and transformation.

So, when we walk with the Spirit, we're not just avoiding sin—we are actively being sanctified. Sanctification means becoming more like Christ, and this transformation affects the same areas where we were once vulnerable to attack:

- The mind that was once tormented is renewed.
- The identity that was once fractured is restored.
- The soul that was once a battleground becomes a sanctuary.

Sanctification teaches us how to *maintain* the freedom that we received in deliverance. It's the daily practice of spiritual health, and like physical health, it requires discipline, nourishment, and community.

Not All Bondage Is Demonic

It's important to remember that not every stronghold is a demon. Some are habits. Some are wounds. Some are lies, and sometimes, we've been so shaped by a mindset of fear or rejection that we assume it must be a spirit.[8]

Scripture teaches that the flesh can be just as destructive as the devil. In Galatians 5, Paul lists the works of the flesh right alongside the spiritual war language of Ephesians 6. The point? We have enemies inside and out.

7. Vondey, *Pentecostal Theology*, 79–80.
8. Lozano, *Unbound*, 40.

The answer to both is the same: submission to Christ and cooperation with the Spirit.

Deliverance deals with the intruder. Sanctification deals with the inhabitant. You can cast out a spirit, but you must *crucify* the flesh. That's why we must teach people how to walk in the Spirit, how to renew their minds, and how to confess truth over their lives. Otherwise, we're setting them up for relapse rather than revival.

Sanctification Is Ongoing, Not Optional

No matter how dramatic the deliverance is, no one graduates from sanctification. It's not a second-tier option for the super spiritual; it's the normal Christian life. We're all in process. We're all being transformed.

While some people may experience instant freedom from addiction, fear, or torment, others will walk out their healing over time. Both are valid. Both are powerful, and both require the church to walk alongside the person—not just celebrating their breakthrough but helping them build their new life.

We need to offer more than altar calls. We need relational discipleship. People who are delivered need *pastors*, not just power encounters. They need truth, not just a testimony. They need help to rebuild what hell tried to destroy.

Freedom for a Purpose

Deliverance is more than a dramatic expression of spiritual authority. It is the entry point into a new way of living. It is freedom that leads to formation.

The man delivered from Legion didn't just get set free—he got sent out. That's what Jesus wants to do for all of us. He liberates us so that we can walk in truth, grow in holiness, and fulfill our purpose.

Freedom is not just about what you walk *away* from. It's about what you're walking *into*. So, let's teach people to fight for their freedom—but let's also teach them how to *live* in it.

Questions to Discuss

1. Why is deliverance only the beginning of a believer's journey toward freedom, and how does sanctification secure what deliverance starts?
2. Forgiveness is presented as essential for sustained freedom. Why do you think unforgiveness is such a powerful foothold for the enemy
3. What role does discipleship play after someone has been delivered from demonic influence, and what are the risks if discipleship is neglected?
4. In practical ministry, how can leaders discern whether a person's ongoing struggles are due to a lack of deliverance, a lack of discipleship, or both?
5. Think of a time when God helped you overcome a spiritual battle. What ongoing disciplines or community support helped you maintain that victory?

Chapter 4

Echoes of Power

If you want to know what a generation truly believed, look at how they lived. The early church didn't just talk about freedom in Christ—they demonstrated it. Deliverance wasn't a fringe practice. It was central to the Christian witness.

They believed that Jesus had already won the decisive battle over demonic powers, and his authority was active through his people. What Jesus began in Galilee, the early church continued in Rome, North Africa, Asia Minor, and beyond. To them, deliverance wasn't dramatic—it was normal.

Chris Hayward writes,

> Ancient writings unilaterally confirm that deliverance from demonic bondage was widespread among believers in the Early Church. . . . Deliverance was so common in the Church that when the apostate Emperor Julian wanted to mock the Christian believers, he ridiculed them for what he identified as the two things marking the essence of their belief and ministry: driving out demons and making the sign of the cross.[1]

In our modern, often sanitized version of faith, we sometimes treat demonology like superstition and deliverance like a rare exception. But for the early church, it was simply part of proclaiming the gospel.

1. Hayward, *God's Cleansing Stream*, 26.

Apostolic Perspectives on the Powers of Darkness

The early apostles did not ignore the existence or influence of unclean spirits. Though the tone and emphasis of their letters differ from the narrative accounts found in the Gospels and Acts, each writer offers important contributions to the church's understanding of spiritual warfare, sanctification, and the presence of evil in the world.

Paul: A Theology of Cosmic Evil and Spiritual Armor

Though Paul does not provide detailed stories of exorcism in his letters, he speaks frequently about the reality of demonic powers. Craig Keener summarizes Paul's contribution well:

> Paul's letters mention his signs and wonders (2 Cor 12:12; Rom 15:19) but do not specify what particular experiences these included. . . Paul is writing letters to the converted, for whom exhortation is more directly relevant than exorcism. The letters emphasize the cosmic role of demonic powers more than Luke-Acts does. . . Paul's letters appear better equipped to address a theology of cosmic evil.[2]

Paul viewed the Christian life as a battle—not just against sin, but against dark supernatural forces. He taught believers to resist evil not only through commands, but through *formation*:

- Spiritual Armor—"Put on the whole armor of God" (Eph 6:11) to stand against the devil's schemes.
- Spiritual Weapons—"We do not wrestle according to the flesh. . . but we have divine power to destroy strongholds." (2 Cor 10:3–5)
- Inner Renewal—"Be transformed by the renewal of your mind" (Rom 12:2) to walk in God's will.
- Peace with God—"Do not be anxious about anything. . . and the peace of God will guard your hearts and minds." (Phil 4:6–7)

Acts provides more narrative detail. Paul cast a "spirit of python" out of a girl in Philippi (Acts 16:16–18) and oversaw a large-scale deliverance

2. Keener, *Acts*, 2464.

and burning of occult materials in Ephesus (Acts 19:11–20).[3] These events demonstrate Paul's authority in spiritual warfare. Yet in his letters, his focus is not on episodic confrontation, but on long-term transformation.

James: Warfare Through Submission

James's pastoral letter calls out behavior that he explicitly labels as demonic—including bitter jealousy and selfish ambition (Jas 3:14–15). However, rather than calling for dramatic intervention, James calls believers to submit to God and to pursue relational and spiritual integrity.

> Submit yourselves therefore to God. Resist the devil, and he will flee from you. Draw near to God, and he will draw near to you. . . Purify your hearts, you double-minded. (Jas 4:7–8)

He acknowledges spiritual warfare, but his strategy is holistic: confession, humility, obedience, and intercessory prayer. When addressing sickness and suffering, James does not associate them directly with demonic influence. Instead, he gives this instruction:

> Let them call for the elders. . . let them pray. . . and the prayer of faith will save the one who is sick. . . confess your sins to one another. . . that you may be healed. (Jas 5:14–16)

Healing, for James, is integrative: involving the spiritual, physical, and communal dimensions of the church.[4]

Peter: Participation in Christ's Victory

Peter's epistles show strong continuity with the Enochic worldview of evil spirits. In 1 Peter 3:18–22, he references Christ's proclamation of victory to imprisoned spirits—an allusion to the defeated Watchers of 1 Enoch.[5]

3. Keener, *Acts*, 2422–29. Keener describes the semantic connection between the "spirit of pythones" and Apollo's Pythian oracle of Delphi. Keener notes on pg. 2429 that John Chrysostom later reads this "narrative as a confrontation with Apollo, here recognized as a demon (*Hom. Acts 35*)."

4. Thomas, *Devil, Disease, and Deliverance*, 5, 12, 22.

5. 1 Enoch 10:4–16; 21:10; see also, Heiser, *Demons*, 115–37, 187, 212.

> Jesus Christ. . . has gone into heaven and is at the right hand of God, with angels, authorities, and powers having been subjected to him. (1 Pet 3:21–22)

Still, Peter's exhortations are strikingly practical. He instructs believers to humble themselves, cast their anxieties on God, and be watchful:

> Your adversary the devil prowls around like a roaring lion. . . Resist him, firm in your faith. (1 Pet 5:8–9)

This balance of cosmic theology and practical resistance demonstrates how deeply Peter understood both the threat and the triumph of spiritual warfare.

His second epistle sounds a sharper note. Echoing themes from Jude and Enoch, Peter warns about those who despise authority and recklessly blaspheme supernatural powers:

> Bold and willful, they do not tremble as they blaspheme the glorious ones. (2 Pet 2:10)[6]

He warns that those who live in rebellion are in danger of being re-entangled in defilement (v. 20) and compares their state to dogs returning to vomit (v. 22).[7] For Peter, sanctification and deliverance are not one-time events; they require vigilance, reverence, and obedience.

Jude: A Warning Against Unholy Associations

Jude's short epistle contains some of the sharpest rebukes in the New Testament. Like Peter, he draws from the Watchers tradition to highlight the danger of demonic corruption among humans.[8] He describes rebellious people as those who ". . .defile the flesh, reject authority, and blaspheme the glorious ones." (Jude 8)[9]

6. 1 Enoch 10:4–16; 21:10.

7. Reddin, *Power Encounter*, 57–58. Reddin notes that backsliders may forfeit divine protection.

8. In addition to other apparent references to the fallen Watchers of Enoch, Jude notably seems to quote directly from 1 Enoch 1:9 in verses 14–15 of his epistle.

9. Heiser, *Unseen Realm*, 331–32. Heiser notes that *doksas*, "glorious ones . . . probably refers to divine beings of the council close to God's glorious presence, since Second Temple period texts describe such beings. . . . The wording suggests some distinction between angels and 'glorious ones" in rank (and perhaps power)."

One of the most intriguing moments in Jude is his reference to the Archangel Michael: "But when Michael the archangel, contending with the devil. . . did not presume to pronounce a blasphemous judgment, but said, 'The Lord rebuke you'" (v. 9). The implication is clear: humility and reverence are essential when confronting spiritual beings. Arrogance in these matters invites judgment.

Jude ends with a call to rescue those trapped in sin: "Have mercy on those who doubt; save others by snatching them out of the fire. . ." (v. 22–23) Even in the midst of warnings, there is grace. Deliverance is possible—but it must be accompanied by repentance, reverence, and dependence on Christ.

An Integrated Theology

Together, these apostolic voices form a deeply integrated theology of spiritual warfare. They do not encourage obsession with demons, but neither do they minimize their reality. Instead, they equip the church to stand firm—rooted in grace, clothed in righteousness, and filled with the Holy Spirit. They do not offer a one-size-fits-all method of deliverance, but rather a Christ-centered life that confronts darkness with humility, wisdom, and the power of God.

Patristic Witnesses on Spiritual Warfare

Justin Martyr: Christ's Authority Is Greater

One of the earliest voices on deliverance we have outside the New Testament is Justin Martyr, a Christian philosopher writing around AD 150. Justin didn't hesitate to describe the power Christians wielded in Jesus's name:

> For numberless demoniacs throughout the whole world, and in your city, many of our Christian men exorcising them in the name of Jesus Christ, who was crucified under Pontius Pilate, have healed and do heal, rendering helpless and driving the possessing devils out of the men, though they could not be cured by all the other exorcists, and those who used incantations and drugs.[10]

10. Justin Martyr, *Second Apology*, chap 7. All citations of early church fathers come from Schaff, *Church Fathers*.

Justin was contrasting the authority of Christ with the ineffective efforts of pagan exorcists. The difference wasn't technique. It was power. Jesus didn't offer superstition—He brought dominion. Justin wasn't just talking about deliverance as a private ritual. He viewed it as a *witness*. For him, the ability of Christians to cast out demons proved that Christ was truly risen and reigning.

However, Justin also went deeper. He connected the origin of demons to the rebellion in Genesis 6—drawing from the Book of Enoch and Jewish tradition.[11] He believed demons were the spirits of the offspring of the fallen angels and human women, creatures corrupted by sin and doomed to roam the earth. He writes that demons,

> subdued the human race to themselves, partly by magical writings, and partly by fears and the punishments they occasioned, and partly by teaching them to offer sacrifices, and incense, and libations, of which things they stood in need after they were enslaved by lustful passions; and among men they sowed murders, wars, adulteries, intemperate deeds, and all wickedness.[12]

Whether we agree with every detail of his interpretation, the point is clear: Justin saw evil spirits as real, personal, and deeply opposed to the kingdom of God. And yet, in the name of Jesus, they were driven out—again and again.

Irenaeus: Deliverance as a Gateway to Discipleship

Irenaeus of Lyon, writing a few decades later, reinforces the same truth. He declared: "For some do certainly and truly drive out devils, so that those who have been cleansed from evil spirits frequently both believe in Christ and join themselves to the church."[13] That progression is vital: deliverance, belief, community. Irenaeus saw deliverance, not as an end in itself, but as the *beginning* of a person's faith journey. Deliverance was evangelistic. It opened hearts to the gospel and brought people into the fellowship of believers. In a world filled with idolatry, demonic influence, and spiritual deception, this was how the church demonstrated that Jesus was Lord.

11. 1 Enoch 15:1–12.
12. Justin Martyr, *Second Apology*, chap 5.
13. Irenaeus, *Against Heresies* 2.37.4. Irenaeus lived from AD 130–220.

Irenaeus didn't treat this ministry as a relic of the apostles' age. He believed it continued in his day—and would continue until the return of Christ. The church was not just a place of teaching. It was a place of cleansing, healing, and spiritual authority.

Cyprian: Baptism as Spiritual Warfare

Fast forward to North Africa in the third century AD, and we find Bishop Cyprian of Carthage describing deliverance in a sacramental context. For Cyprian, baptism wasn't just a symbol of new life—it was an *act of spiritual warfare.*

He describes how, during the preparation for baptism, demons would resist violently. He says they were "scourged, and burned, and tortured by exorcists, by the human voice, and by divine power" as they were driven out of those preparing to receive Christ.[14]

Cyprian used powerful imagery:

> When. . .they come to the water of salvation and to the sanctification of baptism, we ought to know and to trust that there the devil is beaten down, and the man, dedicated to God, is set free by the divine mercy. For as scorpions and serpents, which prevail on the dry ground, when cast into water, cannot prevail nor retain their venom; so also the wicked spirits, which are called scorpions and serpents, and yet are trodden under foot by us, by the power given by the Lord, cannot remain any longer in the body of a man in whom, baptized and sanctified, the Holy Spirit is beginning to dwell.[15]

He saw water baptism as the boundary line—where the kingdom of darkness lost its grip, and the Spirit of God took residence.

This is consistent with the apostolic witness. Paul writes,

> having been buried with him in baptism, in which you were also raised with him through faith in the powerful working of God, who raised him from the dead . . . by canceling the record of debt that stood against us with its legal demands. This he set aside, nailing it to the cross. He disarmed the rulers and authorities and put them to open shame, by triumphing over them in him. (Col 2:12–15)

14. Cyprian, *Epistle 75, To Magnus.* Cyprian lived from AD 210–258.
15. Cyprian, *Epistle 75, To Magnus.*

The imagery of baptism includes believers participating in the death, burial, and resurrection of Jesus, through which demons were conquered.

This is consistent with the witness of John's Gospel, where no demons are exorcised from individuals, but assurance is given that Satan himself will be cast out. John writes, "'Now is the judgment of this world; now will the ruler of this world be cast out. And I, when I am lifted up from the earth, will draw all people to myself.' He said this to show by what kind of death he was going to die." (John 12:31–33) Satan is defeated through the cross, and that victory over darkness is symbolized in baptism.

However, it should be solemnly noted that Cyprian also warned against returning to sin after baptism: "[I]f subsequently they begin to sin, [they] are shaken by the return of the unclean spirit, so that it is manifest that the devil is driven out in baptism by the faith of the believer and returns if the faith afterwards shall fail."[16] This mirrors Jesus's own warning in Matthew 12 that when a spirit leaves a person, it may return with seven more if the heart is left empty.

For the early church, baptism wasn't just a ritual. It was a line drawn in the sand—a death to the old, a resurrection into the new, and a public statement of deliverance from Satan's grip.

Chrysostom: Compassion for the Tormented

John Chrysostom, the golden-mouthed preacher of the fourth century (AD 347–407), offers a different but equally valuable perspective. While others focused on exorcism, Chrysostom emphasized compassion and holistic care.

He wrote that demonized persons were "troubled by evil spirits [and] deserve rather our pity and our tears" instead of our anger.[17] For Chrysostom, demonized individuals weren't villains; they were victims. He saw their torment as a form of madness, and he urged the church to respond with gentleness, not judgment.[18]

16. Cyprian, *Epistle 75*, *To Magnus*.

17. Chrysostom, *Homily on Matthew* 27.4.

18. Salem, "*Sanity, Insanity, and Man's Being*," 8. Salem writes, "Chrysostom understood mental illness, 'classic' demonic possession, and sin (which is also truly a type of demonic possession) all as types of insanity. Of the three, sin is clearly the most serious." Chrysostom discusses the three types of "madness" in numerous places, but he does so most prominently in his homilies on Matthew and 2 Corinthians.

Chrysostom did not view demon possessed people as fully responsible for their own actions.[19] By contrast, he noted that those who willfully live in sin "are frantic while they reason, keeping their orgies in the midst of cities, and maddened with some new kind of madness."[20] Chrysostom says he "would sooner consent to dwell with ten thousand demoniacs, than with one diseased in this way."[21] Stated another way, he had more hope for the demonized than he did for compulsive sinners. A demonized person could be healed, but the arrogant, self-sufficient person often refused the grace of God.

Chrysostom also showed a notable openness for his time—he believed that medical treatment had a place in caring for those struggling with mental illness.[22] He acknowledged that not all madness was demonic and encouraged the use of physicians when appropriate. He writes, "[T]he physicians, when they are kicked, and shamefully handled by the insane, then most of all pity them, and take measures for their perfect cure, knowing that the insult comes of the extremity of their disease."[23] This was not a man afraid of mystery. It was a pastor grounded in truth, eager to see people whole—spiritually, mentally, and emotionally.

The Bible's Balanced Perspective

While the early church held a firm belief in the existence and activity of demons—and maintained a strong practice of spiritual deliverance—Scripture itself offers a more nuanced and balanced view than many modern interpretations allow. A biblically faithful perspective neither ignores

19. Although it is debatable to say that demonized people aren't fully responsible for their own actions, authors writing about possession commonly note that demonized people experience a loss of agency, an inability to exercise their own will. Although they are ultimately responsible for their actions in a moral sense, it may not be accurate to assume that people who are deeply demonized are consciously planning out the ways in which they act out toward others. Chrysostom contrasts such people with those who are simply addicted to wrongdoing.

20. Chrysostom, *Homily on Matthew* 28.4.

21. Chrysostom, *Homily on Matthew* 27.4. To clarify, "diseased in this way" refers to those who willfully and compulsively live in sin.

22. Salem, "*Sanity, Insanity, and Man's Being,*" 11; see also Chrysostom, *Homilies on the Second Epistle of St. Paul to the Corinthians* 29.6.

23. Chrysostom, *Homily on Matthew* 18.6.

spiritual influence nor overstates it. Instead, it honors the complexity of the human condition and the diverse ways God brings healing.

One of the greatest mistakes in spiritual care is the tendency to attribute all suffering, particularly psychological or physical illness, to demonic forces. This assumption is neither representative of the early church's theology nor its practice.[24] As seen in both apostolic writings and patristic reflections, early Christians recognized the multiplicity of human affliction. Sometimes, it is caused by spiritual oppression. At other times, it results from grief, physical illness, moral failure, divine judgment, or emotional exhaustion.

The Old Testament, which the early church revered as sacred Scripture, is full of examples of psychological distress without reference to demonic influence:

- **Job** cries out for death after the catastrophic loss of his children, health, and wealth:

  > Oh, that I might have my request, and that God would grant me the thing that I long for! Even that it would please God to destroy me. . . . (Job 6:8–9)

- **Elijah**, after a major spiritual victory on Mount Carmel, longs to die in the wilderness:

  > It is enough; now, O Lord, take away my life. . . . (1 Kings 19:4)

- **Jeremiah**, crushed by prophetic rejection, despairs:

  > Cursed be the day on which I was born! (Jer 20:14)

- **Jonah**, angry at God's mercy on Nineveh, declares:

  > Therefore now, O Lord, please take my life from me, for it is better for me to die than to live. (Jonah 4:3)

These instances reflect "the debilitating contemplation of death characteristic of a depressed state of mind."[25] These prophets and saints were not

24. Thomas, *Devil, Disease, and Deliverance*, 297. Thomas here notes, "In contrast to claims made both at the scholarly and popular levels, the New Testament writers generally make a clear distinction between demon possession and illness."

25. Wohlgelernter, "Death Wish in the Bible," 131.

condemned for their struggles; they were met with grace, divine encounter, and in some cases, correction or comfort.

Scripture also includes cases of psychological breakdown linked directly to divine judgment—but not explicitly to demons. King Saul becomes mentally unstable after the Spirit of the Lord departs from him:

> Now the Spirit of the Lord departed from Saul, and a harmful spirit from the Lord tormented him. (1 Sam. 16:14)

Whether this "harmful spirit" is understood as demonic, metaphorical, or judicial, the emphasis is not on exorcism but on divine sovereignty.[26] Saul descends into homicidal rage and paranoia (1 Sam. 18:10–11), but no record suggests he was offered deliverance.

Nebuchadnezzar, king of Babylon, experiences a complete mental collapse—living like a wild animal for a time—as judgment for his pride (Dan 4:30–33). His condition is neither labeled demonic nor treated through spiritual warfare. Restoration comes through repentance and divine mercy.

Even King David, a man after God's own heart, expresses deep emotional anguish in the Psalms:

> I am languishing. . . my soul is greatly troubled. . . I am weary with my moaning; every night I flood my bed with tears. . . . (Ps 6:2–6)

This prayer is raw and real. It reflects emotional pain, likely depression, but again, not demonic possession.

The Gospels and Acts offer powerful accounts of healing and deliverance—but they too draw careful distinctions. Some conditions are clearly associated with unclean spirits (e.g., the boy with seizures in Mark 9:17–27). Others are healed through forgiveness (Mark 2:5), touch (Mark 5:34), or simple acts of faith (Mark 10:52). Not every sickness is treated as demonic, and not every deliverance requires exorcism.

In other words, Scripture presents a balanced, Spirit-led model of ministry—one that addresses the body, the soul, and the spirit without over-pathologizing or over-spiritualizing. The apostles and early church fathers inherited and preserved this balance. They acknowledged the reality of unclean spirits and practiced deliverance with boldness, but they also upheld prayer, pastoral care, repentance, forgiveness, confession, and medical wisdom as indispensable tools in the healing journey. A faithful deliverance ministry must follow this pattern—not one rooted in fear or

26. The King James Version refers to it as an "evil spirit from the Lord."

oversimplification, but one grounded in Scripture, humility, and the holistic love of Christ.

What We Must Recover

The early church wasn't perfect. They didn't always agree on the origins of demons or the methods of exorcism. But they shared something we desperately need today: a confidence in Christ's authority, and a commitment to healing the whole person.

They weren't afraid of spiritual conflict. They understood that the gospel would provoke opposition. However, they also knew that every time a demon was cast out, it confirmed the truth of Christ crucified and risen.

Deliverance wasn't the exception; it was the expression of a living faith. We must recover their boldness. We must recapture their clarity, and we must embrace their compassion, because the Jesus they preached is the same Jesus we serve. His power has not diminished.

Leah's Testimony: A Fire Where the Chains Once Were

Churches and leaders that embrace Christ's liberating power continue bearing witness to the kinds of testimonies that were normative for the early church. Leah's story illustrates this truth. Leah spent years reaching for freedom without fully grasping it. She came to church often, arms lifted in worship—but her soul was still heavy. Fear, worry, and shame clung to her like invisible chains. Her body showed up, but her spirit struggled. Her eyes remained downcast, and her arms felt like they carried invisible weights.

"I thought I was worshiping, but I was just reaching. There was something holding me down."

Leah reached out to her pastors and shared that throughout her life, she had felt as though she was being tormented by demons. People in her life had even gone so far as to tell her that she had a demon, but she had been left in despair, receiving criticism without loving intervention. Shortly after that conversation with her leaders, everything changed.

One day, during a time of prayer and spiritual ministry, the weight lifted. It didn't happen gradually; rather, breakthrough came suddenly. Leah described the experience like this:

> I felt like a cool breeze went across my whole body and face. . . like a waterfall of peace washed over me. And now, it's like that peace has been replaced with fire. . .I can't even describe it.

For Leah, deliverance didn't just lift the weight; it birthed new desire: a desire to grow, to change, and to step out of survival and into her true identity.

"I feel loved, held, and not empty. I'm not alone. I finally feel what I've been searching for—and God hand-delivered it." She wept—not in fear, but in wonder. "It's like I was walking underwater with weights tied to my hands and feet. And today, I stepped out of the water. The chains are gone. I'm set free."

Leah's awe-filled response is a reminder that sometimes we don't realize how heavy the chains were until they fall off. Her words echo the heart of Isaiah 61:1: "He has sent me to bind up the brokenhearted, to proclaim liberty to the captives, and the opening of the prison to those who are bound."

What happened to Leah wasn't just emotional relief; it was spiritual liberation. What followed was more than joy; it was purpose. It was the fire of holiness where the weight of oppression once stood.

Freedom and Transformation

The early church wasn't intimidated by demonic power because they were anchored in divine authority. They understood that the cross of Christ had broken the back of Satan's dominion—and they lived like it. So should we.

Today's Christ-followers need to reclaim the perspectives of the Apostles. We need Paul's vision of Christ as the one who overcomes cosmic evil. We need to cast out demons, but we must also be ever conscious of Satan's work in many of the world's systems. Imitating Christ in everyday life therefore becomes an act of warfare. Indeed, this is James's clarion call—through active submission to Christ, believers defy the will of demons and Satan flees! Further, people who find themselves in conflict with evil need the Apostle Peter's revelation that believers actively participate in Christ's victory and that it is possible to serve Jesus without falling. Finally, Christians must heed Jude's warning against unholy associations, knowing that the enemy is constantly seeking a way to tear down Christ's church.

Not only do we need the Apostles' perspective, we need to listen to the voices of the church fathers with fresh ears. In a culture that is increasingly saturated with "spirituality," we urgently need Justin Martyr's reminder that followers of Christ uniquely possess what is needed to bring freedom to our society. While academics debate the nature of the supernatural, we need to hear Irenaeus reminding us that the day of miracles has not passed! Cyprian's prophetic vision of baptism as an act of defiance against Satan that topples demonic strongholds needs to be reclaimed by today's church. Baptism is not just a symbol. It is an act of identification with Jesus Christ, and through that act, demons that were unafraid of ritual attempts at exorcisms are overthrown like Pharoah's army in the Red Sea. In an hour when people love to accuse Christians of superstition, we need to regain the golden insights of Chrysostom, who taught people to distinguish between sin, demonization, and mental illness more than a millennia before the rise of the mental health movement.

The history of deliverance is not merely an academic journey through dusty archives; it is the record of a church that knew it must either rise in power or retreat in fear. The same choice stands before us today. Will we compromise the gospel by neglecting the unseen realm, or will we reclaim the boldness of a church that cast out demons in the name of Christ? The stories of yesterday must ignite our faith for today. We are not called to nostalgia; we are called to battle.

Deliverance is not a side-show. It is a natural, healthy expression of balanced gospel ministry. And when we reclaim the truths that the early church carried—truths about identity, cleansing, holiness, and Spirit-empowered freedom—we'll see what they saw:

People set free.

Communities transformed.

And the name of Jesus lifted high.

Questions to Discuss

1. How do the writings of the apostles and early church fathers help anchor deliverance ministry in theological and historical balance?
2. Ephesians 6 describes the armor of God as essential for spiritual warfare. Which "piece" of the armor do you think is most underestimated today, and why?
3. Why is compassion a critical element of deliverance ministry, and how does it differ from a purely confrontational approach?

4. What dangers arise when deliverance ministry disconnects from the broader mission of the church to make disciples?
5. Patristic voices often emphasized Christ's ultimate authority over the demonic. How can reclaiming this emphasis help the church face modern spiritual warfare with confidence instead of fear?

Chapter 5

Pastors in the Crossfire

In today's ministry landscape, pastors are encountering more cases of deep emotional and psychological pain than ever before.[1] Week after week, people walk into our offices and altars with burdens that can't be explained by a single category. Sometimes, what looks like anxiety is really a spiritual attack. What sounds like depression might be rooted in childhood trauma, and what appears to be psychosis may, in some cases, reveal spiritual torment that no pill can touch.

This is the tension we live in. Deliverance ministry cannot ignore the realities of mental illness, but neither can pastors ignore the spiritual dimension of human suffering. We must learn to walk the line. This tension is not new. Paul reminded the Thessalonians to "test everything; hold fast what is good" (1 Thess 5:21). The call to discernment is as urgent now as it was in the early church. To understand the weight of this reality, let's step into the story of one young woman whose life illustrates both the tragedy of trauma and the hope of integrated healing.

1. Wang et al., "Patterns and Correlates," 647; see also, Sutton, *Counseling and Psychotherapy*, 210. Wang et al.'s research demonstrates that when people battling mental health disorders choose to reach out for help, one-fourth will contact a member of the clergy. Sutton's also cites data demonstrating that many Pentecostal and Charismatic Christians have a clear preference for pastoral counseling over psychotherapy or medication.

Nicole's Story: Trauma, Torment, and the Road Back

Nicole's journey reminds us that the human soul is not a clean slate on which life writes evenly. From the very beginning, her story was marked by brokenness. At three years old, the state removed her from her birth home after repeated abuse and neglect. A string of foster placements followed, until she landed in a children's home.

It was there that her heart endured yet another wound. A family had begun the process of adopting her, and hope began to bloom. But at the last minute, they changed their minds. For a little girl already carrying so much loss, the sting of rejection cut deep. By the age of seven, she had already endured more loss than many face in a lifetime.

Not long after, another family came to the children's home to talk about adoption. This time, Nicole's little heart leapt toward them. Within ten days she was living in her new home, suddenly leaving behind nearly everything and everyone she had ever known. Even joy came with a cost. While she embraced her new family with laughter and a larger-than-life personality, the abrupt move was yet another trauma layered on an already fragile soul.

For a season, life seemed steady. Nicole's family called her their "perfect" child—bubbly, mischievous, and full of energy. But trauma rarely sleeps. By her early teen years, waves of confusion rolled over her. She struggled to feel loved, even when love surrounded her. Her dad adored her, but he sometimes missed the desperate cries for help hidden behind her bright smile. Inwardly, Nicole wrestled with questions of gender and sexuality, while outwardly presenting different versions of herself—one for her family, another for her peers, and yet another for the online world of YouTube influencers who quickly became her obsession.

Isolation grew. Depression deepened. Nicole began to hear voices, see shadows, and feel tormented at night. Five times she attempted to take her life. Five times, mercifully, she survived. The torment she described was not simply psychological; it felt spiritual. She was convinced demons were harassing her, and the evidence seemed to support it.

The breaking point came at church camp. During a prayer service, Nicole collapsed to the ground as other voices screamed out of her. When intercessors declared the power of the blood of Jesus, those voices shrieked, "There is no blood!" Yet as repentance was spoken over her and prayers rose up, peace began to break through. Nicole came home testifying, "God set me free." The relief was real. The freedom was real, but the journey was not over.

In time, the torment returned—not always with the same dramatic manifestations, but in subtler, darker ways. Suicidal thoughts persisted. Risky behaviors escalated. In her vulnerability, an older man preyed upon her, leaving her wounded, confused, and filled with rage. Her parents began to realize how many warning signs they had missed. They turned to doctors, specialists, and counselors for help, and they cried out to God with greater desperation than ever before. What they discovered was another layer of the puzzle: Nicole had Hashimoto's disease, an autoimmune thyroid disorder.

For some, Hashimoto's is easily managed. For others, it produces devastating psychiatric effects, including symptoms that mimic bipolar depression, schizophrenia, or even demonic possession. Nicole was among the latter. When she began treatment, the change was nothing short of miraculous. Her vibrant, larger-than-life personality reemerged. Medication did what prayer and deliverance alone had not—it stabilized her body so that her soul could begin to heal.

But healing was not instantaneous. Nicole's relationship with her dad had grown especially strained through the years of confusion, silence, and misunderstanding. Later, when she shared her testimony, she said, *"My dad and I had to hurt each other's feelings and talk about things that neither one of us wanted to talk about."* Those difficult conversations, paired with prayer, counseling, medication, and Nicole's own determination, opened the way to genuine restoration. Today, her passion for life is contagious, radiating to everyone who knows her.

Nicole's story is more than a personal testimony—it is a pastoral case study. It reminds us that trauma leaves lasting scars, that demons often exploit those wounds, and that discernment requires humility. Deliverance brought her real freedom, but medical treatment also played a critical role. Neither was enough alone. It was the convergence of spiritual intervention, clinical care, family honesty, and relentless grace that brought her into wholeness.

Nicole is living proof that the road to healing is rarely one-dimensional. It is not simply about exorcism, therapy, or medicine in isolation. It is about integration—body, mind, and spirit brought under the lordship of Jesus Christ.

Reflection

Stories like Nicole's place pastors squarely in the crossfire. When someone presents with torment, is it trauma? Is it demonic? Is it neurological? Sometimes the answer is yes to all three. To treat every manifestation as purely spiritual is to risk overlooking real medical conditions. To treat every symptom as purely medical is to risk ignoring real spiritual bondage. The cost of misdiagnosis is high, and the lives of vulnerable people hang in the balance.

Nicole's journey demonstrates why pastors must cultivate both spiritual discernment and practical wisdom. We must pray with authority but also partner with physicians and counselors. We must be ready to confront the demonic but also willing to sit with the wounded in long, difficult conversations. Healing is rarely simple. But when body, mind, and spirit are cared for together, the church becomes the place where people like Nicole can finally be made whole.

This brings us to the critical question for every shepherd of souls: *what are pastors called to do when they find themselves in the crossfire between the spirit and the psyche?*

Wounded Souls and Wise Shepherds

Most Pentecostal and Charismatic pastors affirm the reality of demonic influence. We believe that spirits still torment, deceive, and enslave. However, many also admit that they feel under-equipped when it comes to identifying whether someone is demonized or mentally ill. We aren't psychiatrists, but we're still expected to bring freedom. We aren't therapists, but we're called to bring healing.

The challenge is that the symptoms often look the same: voices, fear, isolation, compulsions, emotional volatility. Some of these may be the result of trauma. Some may stem from generational sin. Others may involve a genuine manifestation of evil spirits. And occasionally, it's all of the above.

Without solid discernment, we risk sending the wrong person to the wrong help. Some people in distress are given medication when they need intercession. Others are subjected to exorcism when they really need therapy. This isn't just bad theology. It's pastoral malpractice. James warns, "Not many of you should become teachers. . . for you know that we who teach will be judged with greater strictness" (Jas 3:1). The same applies to shepherds of souls—when we fail to handle people with discernment, the stakes are eternal.

The Cost of Misdiagnosis

One of the most daunting fears for many pastors is misidentifying a serious mental health condition as demonic. Imagine trying to cast out a demon from someone suffering with schizophrenia, only to find out later that their symptoms were entirely psychiatric. Not only is that emotionally devastating—it can erode trust, reinforce stigma, and even open the door to legal consequences.[2]

Some pastors have stepped away from deliverance ministry, not because they lack faith in God's power, but because they feel underqualified to assess symptoms that could be psychological in nature. In truth, that fear is not unfounded. Misdiagnosis carries real consequences.

I've faced this inner struggle myself. In my early twenties, I was praying for people to be set free almost daily. Many experienced miraculous deliverance, but others stayed bound—or worse, became more distressed. That dissonance triggered a crisis of confidence. I stepped back, not because I stopped believing in spiritual warfare, but because I wasn't always sure what kind of help people truly needed.

That season, while difficult, became a turning point. It drove me to study mental health with fresh urgency, seek out wise mentors, and learn the language of trauma and diagnosis. I began counseling more, listening more,

2. Meza, "Multiple Personality Disorder and Demonic Possession," 1; see also, Willis, "Liberation and Integration," 104–7, 163–64. It should be noted that while some mental health professionals are open to multi-disciplinary perspectives, others are not. When evaluating whether someone may be suffering from demonic influence, I find that it is usually helpful to know if they have been diagnosed with a mental illness. However, if their therapist holds to a fully secular worldview, it is possible for people to be diagnosed with a psychological condition when it is truly more spiritual in nature. Meza writes, "An estimable difference was not found in actual experience between those individuals who believed they were possessed by a demon and those affected by . . . a diagnosis of a physically-situated MPD or dissociative disorder." This statement is indicative of Meza's overall thesis. Although he raises valid concerns, I disagree with his assessment. Nonetheless, it is important to know that there are therapists who hold no space for the possibility of spiritual disorders. I offer an analysis of some of Meza's critiques of exorcism in my dissertation, referenced above, which is available as a free download on ProQuest as well as in Academia for those who have an account with them. There are multitudes of highly qualified mental health professionals who champion the importance of incorporating spiritual perspectives into people's healing journey.

referring more. I discovered that not every battle is won by casting out; some require compassionate dialogue, therapeutic intervention, and time.

However, there is another danger: swinging the pendulum too far in the other direction. Avoiding deliverance altogether because of its complexities risks abandoning a core ministry of Jesus. You can't cast out mental illness, but neither can you counsel a demon.[3]

So, what's the answer? Discernment. Partnership. Equipping.

We must become better listeners, both to people and to the Holy Spirit. We must stop pitting theology against psychology, and instead foster collaboration between pastors and professionals. Deliverance is not a substitute for mental health care, but neither is mental health care a substitute for spiritual authority. When we get both in the room—when we bring Spirit-filled discernment alongside clinical wisdom—we're better positioned to help the whole person.

Mistaken Identity: Medical and Psychological Conditions Often Misdiagnosed as Possession

Misdiagnosing a medical or psychological condition as a demonic presence is a legitimate concern for many pastors. While the church must remain vigilant about the spiritual realities of torment and oppression, we must also walk in wisdom—recognizing the complexities of the human brain, body, and psyche. Ignorance in this area does not just lead to embarrassment. It leads to harm.

In this section, we'll examine several clinical and neurological conditions that are frequently mistaken for possession, along with insights from respected deliverance ministers and mental health professionals on how to tell the difference.

Schizophrenia: Disrupted Reality, Not Demonic Occupation

Schizophrenia is one of the most misattributed disorders in deliverance contexts. Hallmarked by hallucinations, delusions, disorganized thinking, and emotional flatness, schizophrenia often includes auditory voices or perceived external commands—features that may resemble possession.

3. I wish to clarify that Jesus can absolutely heal people of mental illness. The intended distinction here is simply that demonization and mental illness are not synonymous and require different kinds of intervention.

Mental Health Therapist Jonathan Seubold explains,

> In everyday life, people are inundated with verbal and nonverbal cues and all kinds of signals that would be too overwhelming to process all at once. The brains of healthy people filter these signals and only bring what is needed into their conscious awareness. People with schizophrenia lose that filter, and their minds are flooded with background noise.[4]

Seubold further explains that there are times when people with schizophrenia cannot trust their senses, so he has to encourage them to ground themselves in other ways. He tells people in his practice,

> If you can't trust your eyes, then rely on your ears. If you can't trust your ears, then believe your eyes. If you're having auditory and visual hallucinations at the same time, sit down and grab hold of a chair, squeezing the chair so that you can focus on something that you know is real. I know it's scary, but it is going to pass. It always passes. You're going to be ok.[5]

Both people with schizophrenia and demonized persons have distressing moments when they hear voices and feel out of control. T. Craig Isaacs offers an important distinction: In true possession, a person experiences a loss of control to an intelligent entity that is not part of the self.[6] In schizophrenia, however, the voices are often chaotic, disorganized, and not externally autonomous.[7]

Isaacs notes that those with schizophrenia tend to maintain a core identity and often recognize their experiences as distressing symptoms, especially when treated. In contrast, people under genuine demonic control often experience an intelligent presence with its own agenda—one that responds directly to the name and authority of Jesus.[8]

Scripture itself recognizes the difference between inner brokenness and external oppression. David lamented, "Why are you cast down, O my soul?" (Ps 42:5), while the Gospels describe spirits that spoke with their

4. Seubold, interview by author, March 18, 2023 in Van Buren, AR. At the time of this interview, Seubold was the division head of children's and adolescent services at Valley Behavioral Health in Fort Smith, AR.

5. Seubold, interview by author, September 14, 2024 at Link Church in Clarksville, AR.

6. Isaacs, *Revelations and Possessions*, 119–25.

7. Isaacs, *Revelations and Possessions*, 124–25.

8. Isaacs, *Revelations and Possessions*, 119–25, 128–44.

own voices and agendas (Mark 1:24). Pastors must discern which cry they are hearing.

Psychiatrist Kenneth McAll documented 150 cases of demonic possession during his clinical career—some of which had been misdiagnosed as schizophrenia. One particularly sobering case involved,

> a married woman in her twenties. She had been diagnosed a schizophrenic and had been passed from one hospital to another. Her last two years had been spent in a padded cell where only her husband had been able to approach her. She had not spoken for two years and was violent. Neither electro-convulsive therapy nor drugs had helped her. In fact, she demonstrated the interesting paradox often seen in these cases, that of responding in the opposite way to drugs, sleeping when given amphetamines, and being wide awake on large doses of barbiturates. When I spoke to her husband, mentioning devil possession, about which he knew nothing, the woman, huddled in her dark corner and dishevelled, stood up and spoke for the first time the name of the possessing spirit and asked to see a priest. She was released and for the past seven years has lived as a normal housewife again and helping her husband in his business.[9]

McAll's observations are a sobering reminder that while schizophrenia is a real and serious mental illness, it is sometimes invoked as a catch-all category for experiences and behaviors that might have other—less natural—explanations. This does not mean that ministers without training in psychiatry should routinely challenge medical diagnoses. However, in rare but serious cases, it is reasonable to look through a broader lens, especially when conventional treatments not only fail but appear to exacerbate the problem or elicit paradoxical responses.

People may hear voices because of schizophrenia or because of demonization. Paying close attention to how the sufferer experiences those voices can be a powerful aid to discernment. The following chart is adapted from Isaacs' writings on the subject.

9. Montgomery, *Demon Possession*, 279.

Do You Hear Voices?

This chart draws its information from T. Craig Isaacs, *Revelations and Possession: Distinguishing Spiritual from Psychological Experiences* (Kearney, NE: Morris Publishing, 2009), 119-125.

	Demonization	Schizophrenia
Voices are incoherent, like a noisy room	No	Yes
Voices are clear, more like a conversation with someone	Yes	No
Hallucinations fade over time	No	Yes
Hallucinations remain clear	Yes	No
Voices and visions are experienced as almost dream-like	No	Yes
Voices and visions have an independent quality that is as vivid as anything else in the surrounding environment	Yes	No
Voices speak about religious or moral issues	Yes	No
Voices keep a running commentary on daily activities	No	Yes
Hallucinations typically do not interfere with processing one's surroundings and experiences.	Yes	No

It is not the role of pastors to diagnose schizophrenia; neither is it the role of psychiatrists to diagnose demonization. As Psychiatrist and Pastor John White writes, "the exorcist has as much right to challenge the doctor as has the doctor to challenge the exorcist with the question: How do you know that such-and-such is the true cause of the patient's difficulties?"[10] Insights like those in the above chart can be enlightening for people in diverse professions, but the best answers are often found through careful discernment and intentional collaboration across disciplines.

Psychiatrist Richard Gallagher adds a crucial layer of nuance to the conversation about mental illness and demonization. He explains:

> It should go without saying that mentally ill patients do not exhibit . . . paranormal traits, though people unfamiliar with psychiatric disorders sometimes imagine so. Such patients obviously cannot levitate, as both Julia and Juan did (or any of the other fifteen or so cases I've either encountered personally or had well verified, not to mention the cases documented in many historical records, like that of 'Robbie Mannheim'). Nor do mentally ill patients possess accurate hidden knowledge. . . . Neither can mentally ill patients or other humans spontaneously start to speak foreign languages expertly without having previously studied them. . . . Finally, though some manic and extremely agitated patients may display a high level of vitriol, energy, and force, they never exhibit anything close in degree to the massive level of preternatural strength or the impossible contortions seen in many possessed individuals.[11]

Gallagher's careful distinction between genuine psychiatric pathology and cases involving paranormal phenomena offers an important safeguard for both pastors and clinicians. Deliverance ministers must exercise humility and restraint, recognizing the value of medical diagnoses, while also remaining open to the possibility that some forms of affliction defy natural explanation. In such cases, discernment and prayer must be paired with pastoral care and, when appropriate, collaboration with trusted mental health professionals.

10. Montgomery, *Demon Possession*, 290.

11. Gallagher, *Demonic Foes*, 83.

Bipolar I Disorder: Extreme States, Not Spiritual Takeover

Another condition frequently misinterpreted as possession is bipolar disorder, especially during manic episodes, which can appear spiritual in nature. Bipolar I disorder is a serious psychiatric condition characterized by alternating cycles of major depressive episodes and full-blown mania. During manic episodes, individuals may display:

- Rapid speech
- Grandiosity (believing they have divine identity or mission)
- Increased goal-directed activity (sometimes religious)
- Reduced need for sleep
- Risky or impulsive behavior[12]

What makes this disorder particularly prone to misdiagnosis in deliverance contexts is its tendency to mimic spiritual zeal or supernatural experience.

Dr. Paul Meier, a psychiatrist and Christian author, notes that hyperreligiosity and loss of control over sex and spending are common symptoms during manic episodes.[13] A person in the grip of mania may claim to be a prophet, hear the audible voice of God, or speak with spiritual authority that feels intense—but disordered. These symptoms do not stem from spiritual empowerment but rather from chemical imbalances in the brain.

Meier details symptoms of bipolar I that may be wrongly interpreted as spiritual in nature:

> Hearing voices that aren't there (auditory hallucinations), and seeing things that aren't there (visual hallucinations) are also common in bipolar I. People can also experience tactile hallucinations (such as feeling bugs crawling all over their bodies) or olfactory hallucinations (such as smelling foul odors); however, these are much less common. When people are manic the voices are usually complimentary and ego-building; their visions will often consist of angels or God. When people are depressed, the voices are almost always derogatory and often tell people to do hurtful things to themselves or others. These are called "command hallucinations." Visions will be of demons, witches or dead people. Most hallucinations are

12. Meier et al., *Blue Genes*, chap 8.
13. Meier et al., *Blue Genes*, chap 8.

> mood "congruent," which means if depressed, they are negative and evil, and if manic, they are positive and spiritual.[14]

In deliverance settings, this poses a dilemma: is this person manifesting a demonic spirit—or simply exhibiting the neurochemical surges of mania?

Here are some key pastoral distinctions to help:

- **Bipolar mania is cyclical**, often following periods of depression and recurring in seasons. True demonic possession, however, does not follow predictable psychiatric cycles.
- **Medication stabilizes** individuals with bipolar disorder, often eliminating psychotic symptoms altogether. Demonization does not typically respond to antipsychotics.
- **Manic behavior is usually self-focused**—centered around personal mission, destiny, or spiritual grandiosity. In contrast, demonic manifestations often center around **defiance**, hatred of the name of Jesus, or contempt for Scripture.
- A person in mania may **quote Scripture** with fervor, but they **do not resist the Word or prayer** in the same visceral way a demonized person often does.

The good news for those suffering from bipolar is that it tends to be very responsive to medication. Meier notes that when people who are experiencing mania and even psychosis check into Meier clinics, they are usually able to stop these extreme symptoms "within a few hours to a few weeks."[15] He continues, "Most patients are able to go home and back to work within three weeks, because they no longer feel suicidal, just somewhat sad still. After ten weeks, 75 percent of them come back and report that this is the best they have ever felt in their lives, or at least in many years."[16] If you are trying to help someone and have reason to suspect that they are suffering from bipolar, the loving thing to do is encourage them to be evaluated by a qualified medical professional.

With the above precautions and suggestions in mind, it is possible for a person with bipolar disorder to also be under demonic influence. Mental illness does not shield people from demonic attack. In such cases, the two realities intertwine, requiring both clinical care and spiritual discernment.

14. Meier et al., *Blue Genes*, chap 8.
15. Meier et al., *Blue Genes*, chap 8.
16. Meier et al., *Blue Genes*, chap 8.

Bipolar disorder is not a demon. Neither are other forms of depression necessarily caused by spiritual oppression. Nonetheless, Meier explains that a holistic approach that does not ignore spirituality is a vital tool for emotional healing:

> Are mood swings always genetic or can they also be psychological or spiritual? The majority of depressive mood swings are due to a combination of spiritual and emotional factors on top of genetic influences. Most people don't get depressed when everything is going well, but rather when a major stressor or tragedy occurs. Unresolved tragedy turns into bitterness, which then becomes a spiritual problem. Unresolved anger creates emotional problems as well. Learning to deal with tragedy and anger through forgiveness and growth brings about increased maturity and wards off depression. Unresolved anger can actually result in serotonin depletion in the brain, thus leading to depression. This is an example of a biochemical problem, triggered by an emotional problem that was brought on originally by a spiritual problem. Depression . . . involves physical aspects, emotional aspects and spiritual aspects.[17]

There will be moments when we are trying to help people and realize that a doctor or counselor needs to be included in the healing journey. This doesn't mean that those without medical or mental health training can't still help. It just means that each of us should stay in our lanes. Distressed individuals may need doctors or therapists, but they also need pastors, friends, and family.

Central Nervous System Lesions: The Brain's Silent Saboteurs

Not all afflictions of the mind are psychiatric. Some are neurological, hidden in the wiring of the brain itself. Lesions of the central nervous system (CNS) are not commonly discussed in spiritual circles, but these can result in:

- Sudden mood changes
- Visual and auditory hallucinations
- Aggression or inappropriate behavior
- Loss of speech or motor function

17. Meier et al., *Blue Genes*, chap 8.

Such symptoms can mimic spiritual attack, especially in cases where the person begins to behave erratically or lose awareness during prayer or worship. However, CNS lesions are often accompanied by physical symptoms (e.g., seizures, tremors, numbness), and diagnostic imaging (e.g., MRI or EEG) can confirm their presence.

A Sobering Case Study

The complexity of neurological illness can easily obscure proper diagnosis—especially when symptoms appear overtly spiritual or bizarre in nature. A compelling example is found in an article published by the *Indian Journal of Psychiatry*, which documents the case of a 43-year-old woman initially suspected of having a "trance and possession disorder."[18] Her symptoms were deeply unsettling and mimicked spiritual possession in ways that could easily deceive even seasoned pastoral counselors.

> She would start shaking her body and head in gyrating movements; she would be unaware of what was going [on] around her [;] she would say that she is sent by her husband's dead sister-in-law to kill her husband; at other times, she would claim that she was a demon. . . . At times, she would utter completely irrelevant and incomprehensible speech.[19]

Such manifestations—gyrating movements, altered states of consciousness, disassociation from reality, the adoption of violent personas, and incomprehensible speech—could understandably lead observers to suspect demonization. In fact, these are hallmark indicators in many deliverance case reports. However, further medical testing revealed that the root cause was a lesion in her central nervous system, not spiritual possession.

This case underscores the critical importance of medical evaluation before initiating spiritual intervention. Deliverance ministers must exercise pastoral responsibility by asking thorough questions, involving qualified professionals when necessary, and understanding that some neurological conditions can closely resemble what the Bible describes as demonic manifestations. This is not a denial of spiritual warfare; it is a call to pursue clarity, integrity, and compassion in the process of discernment.

18. Basu et al., "Trance and Possession," 65–67. The authors here reference "culture bound syndrome," which is another label for possession syndrome.

19. Basu et al., "Trance and Possession," 65–67.

Where there is true demonic activity, the authority of Christ is sufficient. But when the cause lies in a damaged brain or nervous system, casting out a demon will not bring healing—diagnosis and medical care will. For those ministering in the delicate space between the spirit and the psyche, wisdom is not optional. It is a sacred requirement.

Thyroid Disorders

As in the case of Nicole, thyroid disorders may resemble spiritual oppression or mental illness. They can induce altered states of consciousness, disinhibition, or mental confusion. Without clinical awareness, a pastor might interpret these signs as demonic when they are actually metabolic. I routinely encourage people who feel they are experiencing spiritual or psychological distress to ask their physician about running a thyroid panel. Although some medical doctors may question why a pastor would suggest specific medical tests, it is important to be thorough, and most will welcome the opportunity to be involved in collaborative care.

Psychiatrist Paul Meier explains, "If the thyroid hormones are too low, you can have insomnia even though you feel very tired all the time, have dry skin, hair loss, weight gain, depression, serotonin depletion, and even psychosis (loss of touch with reality). If the thyroid hormones are too high, you can get manic and psychotic."[20] Meier recounts the following story:

> I admitted a suicidal college student with severe insomnia into our Day Program. . . . He usually behaved quite normally. At that time, though, he felt demons in various parts of his body and was delusional and couldn't sleep. I couldn't find any significant psychological or spiritual reasons for his psychotic depression, and he had no family history of it. But he did have a family history of thyroid abnormalities, so I ran a series of thyroid tests on him and he had almost no thyroid hormones in his blood. I gave him thyroid hormones daily and some serotonin and dopamine medicines, and he cleared up quite rapidly, back to his normal behavior.[21]

Ruling out conditions of this nature can be an important part of the discernment process. Proverbs reminds us, "The discerning heart seeks knowledge." (Prov 15:14) Recommending medical testing is not faithlessness; it is wisdom.

20. Meier et al., *Blue Genes*, chap 3.

21. Meier et al., *Blue Genes*, chap 3.

The Principle of Rule-Outs and Red Flags

Wise deliverance ministry operates by the principle of discernment, not diagnosis. If a person exhibits possible medical or psychiatric red flags, the minister should pause and recommend clinical evaluation. Some of these red flags include:

- Persistent symptoms that do not respond to prayer
- History of psychiatric hospitalization or trauma
- Physical signs of neurological dysfunction
- No spiritual reaction to the name of Jesus or Scripture
- Resistance to treatment that seems rooted in paranoia
- Long term addiction to mind altering substances or alcohol

Wisdom Is Warfare

When we misdiagnose medical illness as demonic, we dishonor the suffering and diminish our credibility. When we ignore the spiritual realm out of fear of error, we leave the afflicted bound. But when we walk in the Spirit with wisdom, we minister with precision, compassion, and real authority.

Deliverance is warfare, but so is discernment.

Let this be the kind of church we build—one that casts out demons, heals the brokenhearted, and refers wisely when needed. In doing so, we protect the vulnerable and honor the name of Jesus.

Between the Spirit and the Psyche

At the intersection of trauma and torment lies perhaps the greatest challenge for pastors: how do we shepherd wounded souls who also face spiritual battle? Trauma is often the missing link between mental illness and spiritual torment. When you trace a person's symptoms back to their story, you'll usually find a wound. MacNutt estimated that two-thirds of all cases of demonization are trauma-related.[22] That doesn't mean trauma always equals demonization, but it does mean that past pain often opens spiritual doors.

22. MacNutt, *Deliverance from Evil Spirits*, 93; see also Driscoll, "How Catholic Exorcists Distinguish," 182; see also, Ripperger, *Dominion*, 440.

Sometimes the trauma leads to dissociation. Sometimes it invites spiritual torment. Often it does both. When trauma is ignored, deliverance may become ineffective. When trauma is addressed, healing becomes sustainable.

That's why we must see the person—not just the manifestation. Behind every panic attack is a story. Behind every rage episode is a soul, and behind every manifestation is something far more complex than a single label. This is why Paul urged us to "carry one another's burdens, and in this way you will fulfill the law of Christ." (Gal 6:2) Discernment is not about labeling—it's about loving.

Martha's Story: When the Boundaries Blurred

To illustrate how these layers of trauma, illness, and oppression can blur, consider the story of Martha. Martha had developed a growing obsession with the occult. She began researching tarot card readings, even paying for one herself. Over time, she became fixated on the figure of Lilith, an ancient demonic entity associated with rebellion, sexuality, and feminine seduction in various mythological traditions. The deeper Martha went into these spiritual curiosities, the more isolated she became. Though she still attended church, she felt no connection to what was happening around her. Martha eventually withdrew emotionally, mentally, and spiritually.

Martha also began experiencing disturbing physical and psychological symptoms. She regularly heard voices—not internally, but with her ears. She felt detached from her body, reporting that she literally could not feel her skin. Sleep was sporadic. At times she seemed to exist in a different world, responding to stimuli no one else could see or hear. She described vivid mental scenes that were disconnected from reality.

Our team met with Martha multiple times. We prayed. We listened. We discerned. The question wasn't whether something was wrong. It was *what kind* of wrong we were dealing with.

Was this demonic? Psychological? The fruit of trauma? Perhaps, it was all of the above? Slowly, the answer emerged.

Through extended conversation, we came to strongly suspect Bipolar I Disorder, which would explain Martha's erratic behavior, her spiritual confusion, and the blurring of sensual and spiritual boundaries. When we asked if she had ever been diagnosed with a mental health condition, Martha quietly admitted she had been diagnosed with Bipolar I as a young adult—but had since gone off her medication. The onset of her symptoms coincided exactly with the cessation of her treatment.

Then came another layer of revelation—this time, through prayer. While ministering to Martha, one of our team members sensed from the Lord that she had experienced sexual abuse in her childhood. When this was gently brought up, Martha broke down. She confirmed the abuse—but said she had never told anyone.

What we were dealing with was not just mental illness. It was also trauma and spiritual compromise. All three layers were active.

By what can only be described as divine intervention, Martha was able to get in to see a psychiatrist within just a few days. She restarted bipolar medication, and when we met with her four days later, she was noticeably improved. One week later, it was like speaking with a different person. Her eyes were clear. Her thought processes were grounded. She was present.

Several months later, during a worship service, Martha experienced what she could only describe as deliverance. In her words, *"My mind went quiet—for the first time in my life."* Whatever demonic oppression had piggybacked on her trauma and illness was lifted in that moment. It was not loud. It was not dramatic. But it was holy.

Martha's story reminds us of this critical truth: deliverance is not a one-dimensional ministry. Biological, psychological, and spiritual needs are all real, and healing often comes through addressing all of them.

What Deliverance Must Become

The stories and diagnoses shared throughout this chapter point us toward a larger reality: deliverance must be reshaped for the world we live in. Pastoral deliverance is not just about commanding spirits to leave. It's about helping broken people become whole. That means deliverance must be layered and sometimes collaborative. A deliverance team might include a pastor, a mental health coach, some intercessors, and a nurse or medical doctor. Sometimes, it should include a licensed counselor with specialized training in trauma-informed care.

That kind of ministry takes humility. It requires pastors to say, "This is outside my lane, but I'll walk with you until we find someone who can help."

Deliverance must evolve from a spectacle to a process, from a one-time prayer to a journey of healing. It must move from fear-driven avoidance to Spirit-led engagement.

Jesus didn't just cast out demons—He restored dignity. And so must we.

A Call to Courage and Clarity

If you're a pastor reading this, you've probably been there. You've prayed with someone and felt unsure. You've asked yourself, *"Is this psychological or spiritual?"* And maybe you've felt the weight of wanting to help—but not knowing how.

Let me affirm this: you are not alone.

The Spirit of God still guides. The Word still speaks. And the same Jesus who set the captives free in Capernaum still moves in your city today.

But he's calling us to grow. To learn. To equip ourselves with both wisdom and power. To recognize the complex ways sin, trauma, and darkness weave themselves into the human soul—and to bring light into that darkness with truth and grace.

Let us not retreat from the tension. Let us stand in it—with discernment, with compassion, and with courage. "For God gave us a spirit not of fear but of power and love and self-control." (2 Tim 1:7)

Questions to Discuss

1. How can we discern the difference between a mental health struggle and a case of spiritual oppression, and why is it important not to oversimplify either?
2. In what ways can deliverance and clinical therapy work together to bring healing to a person's life?
3. Why is it important to treat those who are suffering with dignity and patience, even when their symptoms are difficult or disruptive?
4. What boundaries should be in place for ministers when working alongside mental health professionals in complex cases?
5. How does renewing the mind (Rom 12:2) play a role in maintaining freedom after deliverance, especially for those with a history of trauma or mental illness?

Chapter 6

Degrees of Darkness

ONE OF THE MOST important lessons I've learned in deliverance ministry is this: not all demonic influence is the same. Some people are tormented by fear at night. Others hear accusatory voices in their heads. Some live under such mental fog that they can't concentrate, pray, or function in daily life. Then there are rare but real moments when a voice speaks from within that isn't theirs—filled with hatred and contempt, cursing and mocking.

What do we make of all this?

In Scripture and in practice, demonic influence exists on a spectrum. Just as physical sickness can range from a sore throat to a terminal illness, spiritual affliction has degrees of severity. Understanding those degrees is key to wise, compassionate, and effective ministry.

A Biblical Pattern of Variation

The New Testament does not give us a technical classification system for spiritual torment. There is no "manual of levels" or glossary of symptoms. But when we look closely, we see that people experienced demonic affliction in different ways:

- Some were deaf and mute. (Mark 9:17–25)
- Some lived in self-harm and isolation. (Mark 5:1–20)

- Others experienced seizures. (Mark 9:18)
- Still others were tormented by "a disabling spirit." (Luke 13:11–16)[1]

These weren't identical cases. Jesus tailored his response to each individual. He wasn't working from a deliverance formula. He was discerning the condition of the soul.

Three Primary Categories of Influence

Based on biblical evidence and contemporary deliverance practice, most demonic influence falls into one of three broad categories:

1. Oppression—External Influence

Demonic oppression refers to a focused external attack from unclean spirits that can weigh heavily on the body, soul, or spirit. Though not the same as possession, it can still be debilitating. Many pastors and ministers have encountered individuals who are overwhelmed by discouragement, shame, anxiety, or unexplained fatigue—symptoms that are not always caused by demons but are sometimes clearly worsened by spiritual harassment.

Oppression is external, but this is not to say that oppressed individuals don't experience internal symptoms. Imagine that a mob of people surround your house and begin beating on the doors and windows. Although the house is locked and the oppressors are outside, you may experience very real feelings of anxiety, panic, and dread. If people continued harassing you for days on end, feelings of anger, bitterness, and even depression might become overwhelming. Oppressed individuals are not inhabited by demons, but that does not make the attack any less real.

1. Williams, "Not Your Average Exorcist," 4–5; see also Reddin, *Power Encounter*, 125–32. Williams omits the woman with a spirit of infirmity from his list of exorcisms, which is indicative of disagreement among scholars over the precise nature of her condition. Reddin, an Assemblies of God scholar, omits the same account from her list of power encounters but does make note of it under a subsection titled, "Other Deliverances." The nature of this account is admittedly different from other exorcisms, as there is no reference to casting anything out and no sort of dialogue with the spirit. Still, the language of Luke 13 seems consistent with a form of demonization, and Jesus explicitly refers to her as one whom "Satan bound for eighteen years" (Luke 13:16). In vs. 11, the ESV says she had a "disabling spirit." The NIV translates it, "crippled by a spirit;" while the KJV states that she had "spirit of infirmity."

Francis MacNutt offers helpful insight into one of the more common manifestations of oppression: emotional heaviness. He writes, "There is what we might call emotional oppression, which comes when our spirit and emotions are weighed down by heaviness or depression. Many human psychological factors produce depression, but sometimes we find a demonic force bearing down on us to slow us up or prevent us from acting. . ."[2] This important observation reminds ministers not to make hasty assumptions. Depression may have natural causes, but demonic influence can exploit emotional vulnerabilities and amplify them. This interaction between the psychological and the spiritual often resists neat categorization.

Chris Hayward echoes this complexity in *God's Cleansing Stream*, especially as it pertains to believers. He explains, "Once indwelled by the Holy Spirit, a Christian cannot be possessed in his or her spirit by a demon. However, his or her soul (i.e., mind, will, and emotions) can be demonically harassed in many ways and with varying degrees of torment."[3] While demonic oppression does not overtake the core of a believer's identity, it can certainly target areas of weakness—clouding their mind, attacking their will, or manipulating their emotions.

Hayward further identifies three common entry points for this kind of torment:

1. "**Personal trials**," such as the "thorn in the flesh" described by Paul. (2 Cor 12:7)
2. "**Believing the lies of the enemy**," which can create mental strongholds and distort a person's view of God, self, and others. (2 Cor. 10:4–6)
3. "**Engaging in sinful behavior**," which may open the door for demonic influence. (Eph. 4:27)[4]

2. MacNutt, *Deliverance*, 75; see also, Trice and Bjorck, "Pentecostal Perspectives," 283–94; see also, Sutton, 209. Referring back to Trice and Bjorck's research, Sutton notes that among Pentecostal and Charismatic believers, "demonic oppression or possession was the fourth highest-rated cause out of 32 possible causes of depression. The researchers found the demonic item was linked to a category of causes labeled victimization." Whatever one makes of this data, it is evident that within certain faith traditions, there is at least a perceived link between demonic attacks and some experiences of depression. Sutton also notes that the same group recognized a "variety of biopsychosocial causes such as relationship concerns, financial problems, and chemical imbalances."

3. Hayward, *God's Cleansing Stream*, 31.

4. Hayward, *God's Cleansing Stream*, 31. The portion in bold and quotes in each of the 3 numbered points is drawn directly from this source along with the corresponding

Each of these pathways underscores the need for an integrative model of deliverance—one that addresses external spiritual pressure while also confronting internal emotional wounds and patterns of sin.

Oppression is not merely a nuisance; it is a deliberate effort to derail, distract, and discourage. Unclean spirits rarely succeed in a single blow. Instead, they chip away at peace and purpose—tempting, accusing, exhausting, and overwhelming. If left unaddressed, this slow erosion of well-being can leave a person vulnerable to deeper forms of bondage. Deliverance from oppression involves speaking truth, renewing the mind, and restoring joy.[5] For believers, the most consistent path to freedom is resistance through the Word, prayer, and the strengthening of community support.

As Bottari wisely observed, "Through temptations and persecutions," demons use "oppression to exert pressure on Christians . . . to go back to their old sinful lifestyles."[6] The effects of oppression may be experienced emotionally, physically, or spiritually. In *Unbound: A Practical Guide to Deliverance from Evil Spirits*, Neal Lozano writes, "Many Christians allow for demonic activity in theory but think it has no practical consequence in the life of a believer."[7] The consequences can be serious indeed.[8]

Through oppression, Satan seeks to wear people down to the extent that they willingly submit to his purposes. Oppression can often be addressed through prayer, fasting, Scripture, worship, and deliverance ministry that focuses on breaking agreement with lies and releasing truth. Demons desire to wear believers down to the point that they give up and give in, but by identifying oppression for what it is and confronting it with the truth of God's Word and the power of the Holy Spirit, the oppressed can not only resist—but overcome.

2. Obsession—Internal Strongholds

Here, demonic influence has moved deeper. The enemy no longer just harasses; he manipulates from within. A person may battle crippling

---

Scripture references. The bold font is mine.

5. Lim, *Spiritual Gifts*, 84.

6. Bottari, *Free in Christ*, 88. Bottari references James 4:7 in conjunction with this statement.

7. Lozano, *Unbound*, 42.

8. This research naturally raises questions regarding demonization and believers. For added perspective on this subject, see Appendix C, "Demonization and Believers."

addiction, compulsive behaviors, suicidal ideation, violent impulses, or emotional outbursts they cannot explain. Jonathan Seubold, explains,

> There is a difference between fleeting thoughts and pressured thoughts. Thoughts pass through most people's minds that they wouldn't want everyone to know about. This is not something that should cause deep concern. However, when a thought, like self-harm or suicide, becomes so compulsive that we feel powerless not to act on it, it's time to get help.[9]

Obsession occurs when the enemy exploits emotional wounds, trauma, or habitual sin. He builds a fortress of lies in the mind and emotions. As Paul writes, "The weapons of our warfare . . . have divine power to demolish strongholds." (2 Cor. 10:4)

In these cases, people need more than a quick prayer; they need a process. Often this includes:

- Breaking agreements with sin
- Forgiving others and self
- Renouncing specific lies and spirits
- Inner healing and trauma care
- Ongoing discipleship

This is where deliverance ministry becomes most powerful—and most pastoral. Deliverance processes are addressed at length in chapters 11 and 12.

3. Possession—Severe Control and Manifestation

Possession occurs when a demonic spirit exerts control over a person's body or speech. In these moments, the person may speak in another voice, display supernatural strength, or manifest violent reactions to prayer or Scripture.

In 1894, John Nevius made these observations about severely demonized people in China:

> It may be said in general of possessed persons, that sometimes people who cannot sing, are able when possessed to do so; others who ordinarily cannot write verses, when possessed compose in rhyme with ease. Northern men will speak languages of the

9. Seubold, interview by author, September 14, 2024.

> south, and those of the east the language of the west; and when they awake to consciousness they are utterly oblivious of what they have done.[10]

Nevius's observations are consistent with those that have been reported throughout history across diverse cultures, language groups, and religions. While completing my doctoral work at AGTS, I documented reports of such phenomena as reported by psychiatrists, clinical psychologists, and anthropologists as well as pastors and Bible scholars.[11]

In his counseling practice, Jonathan Seubold has encountered claims of people who levitated and experienced other "psychic" phenomena during times of extreme distress, and I am personally aware of numerous firsthand accounts of objects moving without being touched during exorcisms.[12] While possessed people may display incredible power, they are also deeply tormented. Severely demonized individuals are often suicidal, dealing with constant pain that is unexplained by medical conditions, and enduring consistent psychological anguish. Possession renders people temporarily unable to control their own mind and body, and it is common for paranormal phenomena to occur near them.

This degree of demonization is relatively rare, but it is very real. People often assume that stronger manifestations are evidence of stronger spirits. Neal Lozano offers a different perspective that is consistent with my personal observations. He writes, "I believe powerful manifestations have more to do with the level of infiltration than the power of the demon, how much of the person's life and personality has been entwined with demonic presence."[13] Unclean spirits love to boast about their power, but we should remember that real power belongs to Christ. Scripture assures us that if we will "submit. . .to God" and "resist the devil. . .he will flee from" us (Jas 4:7).

Possession doesn't mean the person is beyond hope or salvation. In fact, many possessed individuals seek help for their condition. While they may feel internally fragmented or lost, there is often a desire for freedom. The goal of deliverance in these cases is not spectacle—it's restoration.

Possessed individuals are often deeply wounded. The enemy gained access through prolonged trauma, occult involvement, or severe sin.

10. Nevius, *Demon Possession*, 51.

11. Willis, "Liberation and Integration," chapter 3.

12. Seubold, interview by author, March 18, 2023.

13. Lozano, *Unbound*, 42–43.

Deliverance must be paired with healing, discipleship, and community restoration.

Where Most People Fall

In my experience, most people who come for help fall somewhere between oppression and obsession. They aren't possessed, but they are affected. They aren't overtaken, but they are tormented.

Many of them are also believers in at least some sense, and this can further complicate the process of accurate assessment. A born-again Christian whose life is actively submitted to Christ cannot be *owned* or *controlled* by a demon, but they can be *influenced*. Just as Christians can sin, become sick, or experience emotional trauma, they can also come under demonic attack or influence when there is unrepented sin, unresolved wounds, or unbroken agreements with darkness.

We must stop thinking in all-or-nothing categories. The truth is that most people are somewhere in between.

Why Classification Matters

Understanding these degrees matters because it prevents two common errors:

1. Misdiagnosis

Some well-meaning ministers treat everything like a demon. If someone has anxiety—it's a spirit of fear. If someone has depression—it's a spirit of heaviness. If someone's child has autism—it must be a generational curse.

This leads to damage. It alienates hurting people, and it misses the real needs of the person in front of us. At the same time, others dismiss everything as psychological. They refuse to consider spiritual warfare, even when the signs are unmistakable. That too leads to bondage.

2. Mismatched Ministry

If we treat obsession like oppression, we offer simplistic answers to deep problems. If we treat possession like obsession, we may place people in danger by failing to engage at the right level of authority. Discernment allows us to meet people where they are, with the tools they need, in the grace and power of Jesus.

Discernment Is Not Guesswork

You don't have to guess which category someone falls into. The Holy Spirit will reveal what's needed as you listen to the person's story, pray with them, and pay attention to patterns.

Here are some practical markers:

- **Oppression** often lifts during worship, prayer, or fasting.
- **Obsession** often persists until lies are broken and emotional wounds are healed.
- **Possession** manifests during spiritual confrontation with speech, body movement, or vocal outbursts that do not originate from the person.

Don't rush to label. Don't be afraid to wait. The Holy Spirit will lead if we are willing to listen.

Mary's Story: When the Storm Is Inside You

For as long as Mary could remember, her mind was never quiet. It was as if twenty different voices were vying for attention in her head at any given time. She struggled to concentrate, yet when something did capture her focus, she became obsessive. Her thoughts were relentless. Loud. Overwhelming.

Mary lived with frequent anxiety attacks and battled suicidal ideation. Her doctor prescribed medication for anxiety and depression, which helped at times, but never brought full relief. The symptoms would intensify around her monthly cycle, though they never fully went away.

She confessed to often experiencing what she called "unholy thoughts"—intrusive images or ideas she never acted on but couldn't seem to escape. She longed to shut it all off. Her preferred escape came through video games and prolonged zoning out, sometimes for hours. She felt numb, disconnected—like she was losing touch with reality.

Things worsened over the course of the year. Mary began seeing a dark figure in her home, and her nightmares intensified. Her husband, a man of prayer, sensed the heaviness in their house as well. One night, the power went out in their home, but the television kept playing for several minutes. The boundary between natural and supernatural had blurred. Mary was spiraling.

The breaking point came when her husband found her curled in a ball in their bedroom closet, wailing and shaking, unable to speak coherently. When they reached out for help, Mary was in severe distress and barely able to engage in rational conversation.

A Window into the Wound

When Mary and her husband arrived for ministry, she was emotionally flooded and spiritually tormented. We spoke gently for a while, but her thoughts jumped erratically. We began to pray.

While interceding, I saw an image in prayer—a little girl, about five years old. I asked Mary, "Did anything significant happen when you were about five?" She immediately began to weep. "I'm not totally certain if I was five," she said through sobs, "but when I was very young, a relative touched me."

She went on to describe sexual abuse she had never before spoken about—not to her husband, not to a counselor, not to anyone. From that point forward, she had felt over-sexualized and ashamed. Her behavior spiraled in youth, and the shame only grew. That shame led to self-hatred, and that self-hatred grew into a death wish. Mary wasn't trying to get attention. She was trying to silence a storm she didn't know how to name.

When the Darkness Manifested

We prayed for quite some time with no apparent shift. Then, led by the Holy Spirit, our team commanded whatever was oppressing Mary to reveal itself in Jesus's name. The atmosphere shifted.

Suddenly, Mary's eyes changed. Her facial features contorted in unnatural ways. Her expression became glassy and bloodshot, as if something else had taken control of her body.

"I'm scared," she cried. "I feel like I'm losing control!"

We rebuked the spirit. She began choking, gasping that she couldn't breathe. Moments later, she was strangling herself, then vomiting, and eventually became incontinent. She screamed. She wept. She shook. She cried that she could see hundreds of eyes surrounding her.

We kept praying, commanding the darkness to leave in Jesus's name. . .and then—peace. The presence of God filled the room. Mary cried out with fresh clarity, *"I see Jesus!"* And she was still.

What Happened Afterward

Mary remembers losing control during that encounter—her body, her voice, her thoughts. Something else had taken over. But after Jesus appeared to her, everything shifted. Inside her mind, it was suddenly quiet.

In the following weeks, Mary was filled with joy. She described an almost surreal sense of peace. The desire for escape vanished. The numbness was gone. She found herself crying in worship—this time, not from fear, but from gratitude.

Importantly, Mary's healing was not limited to a single moment of deliverance. Her breakthrough came as she:

- Faced her trauma for the first time,
- Gave voice to secret pain,
- Gave and received forgiveness,
- Welcomed Jesus into her wounded places.

She also submitted to God and resisted the devil, as James 4 commands—and the demonic obsession broke. The dissociative episodes, which had previously caused her to lose time and disassociate for hours, ended that day.

The Whole Healing Journey

Mary's situation was complex. Strong elements of trauma-based reactivity, frequent dissociation, and spiritual torment were all present. While the encounter had clear indicators of demonic obsession, possibly bordering on possession, it was Mary's shame, secrecy, and soul-fragmentation that created the conditions for darkness to take root.

After her deliverance, our team encouraged her to continue healing through counseling. We also recommended a medical evaluation, particularly to rule out hormonal imbalances or cyclical neurological conditions, since she noted her struggles often intensified with her cycle.

The trauma Mary endured didn't vanish overnight. But the hold it had on her soul. . .that broke when Jesus stepped into the memory, and Mary stepped into the light.

From Diagnosis to Destiny

Classifying the degree of spiritual influence isn't about reducing people to a category—it's about equipping us to care for them more wisely.[14] Every person in torment is more than a case. They are a child of God, made in his image, and destined for freedom.

Understanding whether someone is oppressed, obsessed, or possessed helps us avoid assumptions and offer ministry that is both compassionate and strategic. It's not an academic exercise—it's a pastoral necessity.

No matter the depth of the struggle, the destination is always the same: restoration in Jesus Christ—the One who heals, redeems, and breaks every chain. So let us minister with boldness and tenderness, with discernment and humility. For in the presence of his light, even the deepest darkness trembles. In the end, what matters most is not the category—but the cross.

Questions to Discuss

1. How does understanding the difference between oppression, obsession, and possession help prevent misdiagnosis in deliverance ministry?
2. Why is it important to recognize that demonic influence exists on a spectrum, and how does this perspective change the way we approach people in need of ministry?

14. Sutton, *Counseling and Psychotherapy*, 210. Sutton explains that if the client believes they are being tempted by evil, then the "solution to the problem becomes one of helping the Christian resist temptation by wearing God's armor of protection from evil." However, if the issue is believed to be oppression or possession, then "the solution is deliverance or exorcism depending on the client's specific faith tradition."

3. Mary's story shows the intersectionality of trauma, psychological symptoms, and spiritual torment. How can ministers partner with counselors, medical professionals, and the Holy Spirit to address all three?
4. Oppression, obsession, and possession each have unique signs. How might discernment and patience in ministry protect both the person and the minister?
5. In your experience or observation, what spiritual disciplines and community practices most help people resist and recover from ongoing oppression or obsession?

Chapter 7

Pathways to Demonic Distress

DEMONIC TORMENT DOESN'T HAPPEN in a vacuum. It's not random. The enemy is opportunistic—but not omnipotent. He looks for doors that have been opened, legal ground that grants him access, and emotional wounds he can exploit.

If we want people to experience lasting deliverance, it's often helpful to identify *why* their torment began in the first place. The Bible, research, and ministry experience consistently point to three major doorways through which people come under demonic influence: personal sin, trauma, and involvement with the occult.[1] Each doorway may look different, but they all lead to the same outcome: torment, bondage, and disconnection from God's presence. Deliverance that doesn't address these doors is sometimes incomplete.

In a moment, we will explore these pathways to demonic torment in greater detail. First, let's take a look Rose's story. As you read, notice how

1. Driscoll, "How Catholic Exorcists Distinguish," 181–82; see also, Appleby, *It's Only A Demon*, 175. Driscoll's insights are drawn from the consensus of the exorcists interviewed for his dissertation. On page 181 they note three possible roots of demonic possession: personal sin, occult activity, and trauma. Driscoll's comments on these pages reveal that he also sees personal sin as a possible root of some mental illness. Appleby adds a fourth category: "Hereditary Curses and Afflictions." Appleby's fourth category is relatively common among deliverance ministers. While an argument can be made that generational patterns of sin impact people, I find Driscoll's three pathways to represent more of a consensus view and is consistent with my own experience and research.

multiple factors converged to create a spiritual crisis, paying special attention to how God worked to bring freedom and healing in her life.

Rose's Story: The Long Road Home

Rose was about thirty years old when she first reached out for help, though her descent into torment began much earlier. Her childhood had been fractured. Raised by her grandparents due to both parents' drug addictions, Rose found little refuge at home. Her grandmother was often harsh, and though her grandfather was her anchor, the chaos around her left lasting wounds.

As early as she could remember, anxiety and depression had gripped her. She kept it at bay for a while by staying busy, but everything unraveled when she turned nineteen. That year, her mind grew darker. She began self-harming, unable to shake a voice that whispered, *"You're not good enough."* She didn't want to die—but she didn't want to keep living like that either.

In that season of despair, Rose turned against her boyfriend—now her husband—lashing out at him emotionally and doing whatever she could to hurt him. She wasn't trying to be cruel, but something inside her *wanted* pain. Her own. His. Anyone's. Eventually, she found herself addicted to meth, using intravenously.

Rose recalls the feeling of hopelessness, "I just felt like the devil finally got what he wanted—me all to himself." Her children were taken from her, and the voices in her head became her only companions. By her own account, she was *"gone."*

An Unplanned Intervention

Despite all this, Rose eventually began attending church again—and that year, she got her children back. She knew God had spared her, and she tried to walk the right path. For a time, she did.

Several years later, life tragically unraveled again. She relapsed. The voice returned, now more demanding than ever. One night at a rodeo, she turned to her husband and said, *"I'm leaving."* She didn't even know why—only that the craving had become louder than her convictions. She walked away from her family, her horses, and everything she loved in search of her fix.

But God intervened.

"Don't ask me how," she later said, "but I guess God was driving my truck. I ended up at my church. It was a Saturday, and there's no church on Saturday—but my pastor and his wife were there for some reason. . ."

I was at the church that night with a few others, cleaning. Rose called in tears, asking for prayer. Minutes later, she walked into the sanctuary. I was standing between two rows of chairs with a vacuum in my hand when she approached. I placed my hand on her shoulder and began to pray.

Immediately, her body was thrown to the floor, and she began violently manifesting. A demonic spirit had taken hold, and everyone present joined in rebuking it. For more than thirty minutes, the battle escalated. At one point, she appeared unconscious and unresponsive, as though even her will had been bound. We anointed her with oil and splashed blessed water on her head.

Suddenly, her eyes shot open. The spirit spoke through her with chilling clarity—declaring violent, homicidal intent. We commanded the spirit to be silent and began speaking to Rose—calling her back into agreement with the Word of God. We led her to forgive her husband and several others. As she forgave, the unclean spirit left in the name of Jesus, and Rose was delivered.

What Rose Remembers

Rose recalls, "All I remember is walking in, and it's like my body just did what it wanted. I somewhat remember pastor praying for me, and then it's like something was in me. It scared me, but I couldn't stop it. It was like vomiting—when it just keeps coming out and you can't control it. I felt my body slithering across the floor. I was watching myself, but I couldn't stop. It was evil. It was scary. But I knew—I didn't want that in my mind or body anymore."

Rose described out-of-body awareness, a hallmark of dissociation, yet the spiritual force controlling her was not a fractured part of herself—it was foreign, malicious, and intelligent. She had a demon, and she knew it.

After the deliverance, she was too weak to walk. I asked, *"Do you want me to call your husband?"* She could barely answer through tears. Still, her heart was free.

"I felt a big relief, like something that had been holding me down wasn't there anymore. The bad thoughts and the addiction were gone. After that day, I haven't felt the same.

I feel like I have a clear picture of life now. I had a lot of hate and scary thoughts—but I thank my Jesus today for saving me. I'm so blessed to know Jesus. He saved me when I was at the end of my rope."

Deliverance and Restoration

Rose was freed from addiction and restored to emotional and spiritual clarity. What happened to her was not a panic attack or dissociative break—it was a case of demonic possession. Her behavior, speech, physical manifestations, and lapses in consciousness all confirmed that a spiritual personality had taken control of her body and mind.

That possession was driven by years of trauma, generational addiction, self-hatred, and bitterness. Rose had opened doors she didn't fully understand. And yet, Jesus came to close them.

Rose's deliverance reminds us that healing is not an abstract doctrine but a lived reality. Her freedom was forged in the collision of compassion, discernment, and the power of Christ. We must not relegate such stories to the margins or explain them away with clinical terms alone. Instead, we must step into the mess, listen to the wounded, and carry them to the cross. If Rose can be restored, so can the many who fill our pews in silence. Her story is not just hers—it is our call to action.

Not every case looks like hers, but when they do, we must be ready. A key aspect of this readiness is understanding how demons gain control in people's lives. Let's take a closer look at some of the most common pathways to demonic torment.

1. Personal Sin—Agreement with Darkness

A common doorway to demonic influence is unrepented sin. This is the category most pastors recognize, and for good reason. Sin is rebellion against God. It invites the kingdom of darkness to take root in our lives.

Paul wrote plainly:

"Do not give the devil a foothold." (Eph 4:27)

That verse appears in a chapter about anger, bitterness, slander, and sexual immorality. Paul isn't just talking about Satan worship. He's talking about unforgiveness and gossip.

When we sin persistently and unrepentantly, we give the enemy access to our emotions, thoughts, relationships, and physical well-being. Sin gives demons a legal claim. They traffic in the areas we refuse to surrender.

Some of the most common sin-related doorways I've encountered include:

- Sexual immorality (including pornography, sexual promiscuity, and adultery)
- Hatred and unforgiveness
- Chronic lying or deception
- Substance abuse and addiction
- Manipulation and control

The longer these sins remain unconfessed, the more ground the enemy gains. In some cases, sin originates with a wound, but when it remains unaddressed, it creates a spiritual breeding ground for oppression.

The link between personal sin and spiritual vulnerability is not merely theological—it is deeply psychological and pastoral. Bottari notes that "the consequences of sin are bondage, a broken heart, oppression, and captivity."[2] When individuals continually act against their own conscience and moral convictions, it creates an internal rupture that leaves them vulnerable on multiple levels. This is what Isaacs refers to when he writes, "There can be a spiritual sickness because of personal sin: the person has gone against the law of God and so has lost the directing power toward wholeness that the Spirit can give to the soul."[3]

Mike Driscoll, reflecting on how Catholic exorcists approach this issue, points out that while the vocabulary between moral theology and psychology may differ, "there is much overlap regarding patterns of sin being a cause of problems in both realms."[4] This overlap is significant. People who live in persistent sin often develop compulsive behaviors, self-destructive thought patterns, and deep psychological turmoil. As time goes on, the spiritual damage affects the body and mind as much as it does the soul.

Chad Ripperger, in *Dominion: The Nature of Diabolic Warfare*, offers one of the most incisive analyses of how sin disfigures the human mind. He writes:

2. Bottari, *Free in Christ*, 62.
3. Isaacs, *Revelations and Possessions*, 112.
4. Driscoll, "How Catholic Exorcists Distinguish," 182.

> In effect, every time we sin, we diminish the intellect's ordering toward prudence, which is the virtue which knows the right thing to do at the right time to attain the right end. . . . [T]he will cannot will evil in itself but only under the appearance of good, when the object of conscience is presented as something sinful. . . . [T]he will moves the intellect to engage in an act of ignorance and error in which it ignores the evil and only looks at the object by considering it under the aspect of the good, which is not what it truly is. . . . [W]e do violence to our intellect every time we choose something sinful.[5]

In simpler terms, Ripperger affirms that sin corrupts the very faculties God gave us to discern truth from error. The result is spiritual blindness and a weakened conscience. Lozano echoes this in *Unbound*, noting, "We have all internalized lies from the master of deception. . . . As a pattern of thinking is built based on the foundational lie, he finds a place to dwell and exerts greater influence on our emotions and will."[6] Personal sin fosters deception. That deception cultivates emotional and mental distress, and that distress may, in certain cases, open the door to demonic influence.

The only remedy is *repentance*. When we confess sin, renounce it, and receive Christ's forgiveness, the enemy loses his claim. Sin is what opened the door. Grace is what slams it shut.

2. Trauma—When the Wound Becomes a Welcome Mat

While sin opens doors by choice, trauma opens doors by pain.[7] Many people who are demonized did *not* choose it. They were victims—of violence, abuse, rejection, or neglect. And in their moment of deepest wounding, the enemy crept in.

When a person is traumatized, a fracture occurs in their soul.[8] That fracture can become a foothold for the enemy. Psychologists call this dissociation. Deliverance ministers sometimes call it fragmentation. Both are

5. Ripperger, *Dominion*, 438–39.

6. Lozano, *Unbound*, 40.

7. Van der Kolk, *Body Keeps the Score*. Although Van der Kolk's book is not about demonization, it is one of the most important books ever written on trauma and how it impacts people in every dimension of life.

8. Bull, *Phenomenological Model*, 137.

describing the same thing: a wounded part of the person splits off, and in that vulnerable state, a spirit may attach.

This doesn't happen in every trauma situation—but it happens more often than we realize. Abuse. Abandonment. Sexual assault. Constant terror. When these things happen, the soul cries out for help, and if Jesus isn't invited in, something else may assume control.

Psychiatrist M. Scott Peck's reflections on one of the two exorcisms he conducted during his career offer compelling insight into how trauma and deception can intertwine. In a follow-up counseling session with a woman who had undergone deliverance, Peck discovered that she had been sexually abused by her father. However, she had constructed a mental narrative that reframed the abuse, convincing herself it wasn't real.[9] Her defense mechanism was not unusual; survivors of trauma often build internal scaffolding to shield themselves from the weight of truth.

What made this case particularly noteworthy for Peck was the spiritual implication he observed in her response. He writes, "I repeatedly told her that God is truth, and truth is what is real. The choice to believe her father's lie because it was the less painful alternative was a choice to believe unreality. And unreality belonged to the devil."[10] While readers may differ in how they interpret this assessment, the essential point remains: trauma often fractures the soul's perception of truth. The internal world becomes warped, and what begins as self-protection can evolve into self-deception.

In this light, Peck's interpretation underscores a critical theme—when trauma leads individuals to embrace falsehoods to survive, the resulting disconnection from truth can open them up to profound spiritual and psychological distress. Whether or not one adopts his exact conclusions, it is indisputable that trauma distorts reality and often creates fertile ground for fear, fragmentation, and spiritual vulnerability.

Trauma-based demonization doesn't mean the person is weak or sinful. It means they were unprotected. In fact, many deeply tormented people are highly sensitive, spiritual individuals who were crushed before they had a chance to grow.

The answer here is not just casting something out. It's *healing the wound.* Jesus comes to bind up the brokenhearted. When the heart is healed, the enemy's strongholds crumble.

9. Peck, *Glimpses of the Devil*, 77.

10. Peck, *Glimpses of the Devil*, 83.

3. Occult Involvement—Agreements with Darkness

The third major doorway is the occult. In this case, the invitation is often direct, even if unintended. Occult involvement includes any attempt to access supernatural power or knowledge apart from God. In our modern culture, it's more common than most people think.

Tarot cards. Ouija boards. Witchcraft. Sage burning. Manifestation rituals. Psychic readings. Spirit guides. Energy healing. Crystals. Astrology. For many people, these are just games or self-care, but spiritually speaking, they are covenants.

Moses warned Israel clearly:

> Let no one be found among you who practices divination or sorcery, interprets omens, engages in witchcraft . . . . (Deut 18:10)

Why? Because all these practices involve calling on spirits other than the Holy Spirit. And those spirits are real—and dangerous.[11]

In my experience, involvement in the occult almost always results in deeper bondage and faster deterioration of mental, emotional, and spiritual health. Sometimes it starts with curiosity. Sometimes it's done out of desperation. Either way, it gives the enemy authority.

Occult involvement continues to be one of the most common gateways to spiritual bondage. Gabriele Amorth, former chief exorcist for the Vatican, claims to have performed over 100,000 exorcisms during his lifetime and attributes more than 90 percent of the possessions he encountered to involvement with the occult.[12] This staggering claim highlights how seriously occult activity is regarded by experienced deliverance ministers. T. Craig Isaacs summarizes this dynamic well: "One of the most common explanations for possession today lies in a person naively approaching evil or the arcane powers of the universe. Many people who are seen to be either

11. MacNutt, *Deliverance*, 91. MacNutt notes that occult spirits only account for 10 percent of what he deals with in deliverance ministry. However, he also states that "they are the most difficult, dangerous group—the true demons from Hell."

12. Amorth, *Exorcist Explains the Demonic*, 79. While Amorth attributes these possessions to the occult, he does not necessarily attribute this occult activity to the afflicted individual in every case. Amorth writes at length about the phenomenon of curses, but he nonetheless attributes the issues cited above to "some spells or evil eye."

oppressed by demons, or to be possessed, have taken part in some aspect of the occult. . . ."[13]

Psychiatrist Richard Gallagher draws a similar conclusion in his medical documentation of a confirmed possession case. Of his patient Julia, he writes, "Julia revealed a long, disturbing history of involvement with explicitly Satanic groups (an obvious, historical antecedent to her then-present condition and to her accompanying 'psychic' abilities, as they might be characterized)."[14] The phrase "an obvious, historical antecedent" implies that for trained observers, the correlation between occult engagement and spiritual harassment is self-evident.[15]

Yet the relationship may be more complex than cause and effect. Psychiatrist Basil Jackson raises a critical question: might there be personality structures that predispose individuals toward occult involvement—and consequently toward spiritual or psychological breakdown? He observes,

> In connection with the current interest shown in occult activity in this country, I have noted that there is an increased tendency for attraction to the occult in those Christians who have a basic paranoid personality structure. . . . I have noted that Christians who claim to be soundly evangelical and who demonstrate this particular personality position often become fascinated with the occult . . . Another question we must ask concerns the relationship between participation in occult activities and the possibility of subsequent demonization or, perhaps, subsequent psychiatric decompensation.[16]

Jackson's reflections underscore the complex interplay of personality, curiosity, and spiritual danger. While occult practice undoubtedly opens individuals to spiritual influence, there may also be psychological or dispositional factors that draw people toward these practices in the first place. The result is a reinforcing cycle of vulnerability and oppression.

Whether by deliberate invitation, inherited influence, or naïve curiosity, occult activity remains a common pathology in cases of spiritual distress and demonization. The path to freedom often begins by recognizing this danger and cutting ties completely.

13. Isaacs, *Revelations and Possessions*, 115.

14. Gallagher, "Case of Demonic Possession," 23.

15. Gallagher, "Case of Demonic Possession," 23.

16. Montgomery, *Demon Possession*, 268–69.

A powerful tool for breaking this kind of agreement is *renunciation.* The person should say out loud:

- What they participated in
- That they reject it completely
- That they now belong to Jesus alone

Renunciation isn't legalism; it's spiritual eviction. It breaks ties, cancels agreements, and severs contracts. It's hard to overstate the danger of occult involvement and the importance of renunciation. These realities are clearly seen in the life of Catherine.

Catherine's Story: From Generational Witchcraft to Glorious Grace

Catherine never chose witchcraft. She was born into it. For generations, her family had practiced various forms of magic—not always openly, but routinely. It wasn't something they sat down to explain. It was simply what they did.

Every birthday came with a ritual: a personal tarot reading. It was a family tradition—celebrated and anticipated. There were candles, whispered intentions, and a sense of mystery that Catherine found intriguing, even comforting.

However, there was always a darker side. Whenever the adults needed privacy for "certain activities," the children were warned: *"Go to your room. If you come out, the witches will get you."* The words were intended as discipline—but they carried real terror. Catherine remembers seeing a witch-like face staring into her room during one of those nights. It wasn't imagination. It was fear incarnate.

Then came the memory that never left her. There were whispers in her family—rumors that her grandmother had once sacrificed a child to Satan. It sounded outrageous, something you might expect in a horror film. Still, Catherine couldn't dismiss it, especially after one terrifying encounter.

She was still a child when her grandmother, frail and aged, burst into their home, screaming that she was going to sacrifice them. She chased Catherine and her siblings with a knife, yelling Satan's name. Her mother rushed to shield them, locking the children inside. But the old woman ripped the door off its hinges—a frail frame suddenly empowered by something unnatural. Only by the grace of God did everyone survive.

The memory haunted her. Still, Catherine saw herself differently. She wasn't one of *those* witches. She didn't cast curses or summon harm. She called herself a "good witch." Her spells were for healing, attraction, peace. So, when Christian friends told her she needed Jesus, she took offense. She didn't see herself as broken or dangerous. She believed she was spiritual, in control, and helping others.

Then one day, everything began to shift. A friend gave her a Bible for her birthday. At first, she was insulted. What was she going to do with that? Nonetheless, the gift planted a seed. During the Christmas season that year, Catherine agreed to go to a church service. It was there that she encountered a love and presence she had never known.

That night, she surrendered her life to Jesus Christ. The change was immediate. Her heart softened. Her priorities shifted. She was filled with peace.

The weeks that followed were marked by deep spiritual warfare: emotional upheaval, nightmares. . .panic. A battle for her soul had begun long before she gave her life to Christ, and now that battle was in full force.

God began to reveal that lasting freedom would require renunciation. She needed to reject the spells she had cast, the rituals she had performed, and the spiritual alliances she had once claimed as innocent. One by one, she surrendered those ties. She repented. She broke agreements. She asked Jesus to cleanse her soul.

The sanctification she experienced in that process was more glorious than words can express. The torment hadn't entered her life through one avenue alone. There were layers of access—generational sin, occult involvement, and wounds from trauma. The darkness entered from many directions, but Jesus drove it all out.

Today, Catherine walks in freedom. The tarot cards are gone. The fear is gone. The title she wears now is not "witch," but daughter of the King. Her story is a radiant testimony that no background is too dark, and no bondage is too old for the saving, sanctifying, delivering power of Jesus Christ.

Closing the Doors for Good

It's not enough to identify the doorways. We must often walk people through the process of closing them:

1. **Sin** must be confessed and repented of.
2. **Trauma** must be brought into the healing light of Christ.
3. **Occult ties** must be renounced and replaced with truth.

Here's what's amazing: *Jesus walks into every one of these doorways with power and compassion.*

- For the one bound by sin, He offers forgiveness.
- For the one tormented by trauma, He offers healing.
- For the one entangled in darkness, He offers light.

No matter how the enemy came in, Jesus knows the way out.

Truth, Grace, and Spiritual Authority

Demonic distress rarely emerges from nowhere—it is invited, often unintentionally, through unhealed wounds and doors left open. The good news of the gospel is that no one is beyond the reach of God's grace. Whether the entry point was sin, trauma, or the occult, Christ offers a greater covering.

Deliverance is not just about identifying where the darkness entered; it's about closing those doors for good—through repentance, forgiveness, and the authority of Jesus.

As we move forward, let us approach the spiritually afflicted not as problems to be solved, but as people to be loved—inviting them into a process where truth disarms deception, grace lifts shame, and the power of the Holy Spirit breaks every chain.

Questions to Discuss

1. How does the concept of "open doors" help explain why demonic torment occurs, and why is it important to identify these entry points during deliverance ministry?
2. Personal sin is often seen as the most obvious doorway, but we sometimes fail to acknowledge that this also includes sins like gossip and unforgiveness. Why do you think these "less obvious" sins still allow torment to occur?

3. Trauma can create a "fracture" in the soul, becoming a foothold for the enemy. How should the church minister to trauma survivors in a way that addresses both emotional wounds and potential spiritual oppression?
4. Occult involvement is described as making direct agreements with darkness, sometimes without full awareness. What practical steps can someone take to renounce and break free from these ties?
5. Catherine's and Rose's testimonies illustrate different combinations of open doors—generational sin, trauma, addiction, and occult ties. What do these stories teach us about the need for personalized ministry approaches rather than one-size-fits-all solutions?

Chapter 8

The Intersectionality of Dissociation and Demonization

In the world of deliverance ministry, few areas demand more wisdom and tenderness than discerning the difference between dissociative disorders and demonic influence. When someone blacks out during worship, speaks in a foreign voice, or collapses under the weight of unseen forces, we're often left asking: *Is this psychological? Is this spiritual? Could it be both?*

We live in a fractured world, and many people bear the invisible scars of trauma. Some fragment to survive pain too deep to face head-on. Others, knowingly or unknowingly, open doors to spiritual darkness. In some cases, both realities overlap—creating a complex storm of suffering that may involve dissociation, demonization, or both. These situations cannot be addressed through simplistic answers or one-dimensional approaches.

In this chapter, we will journey into the clinical landscape of Dissociative Identity Disorder (DID) and Dissociative Trance Disorder (DTD)—two diagnoses that often resemble the kinds of spiritual torment historically described as possession. We'll also examine the broader phenomenon of possession syndrome across various cultures, and how mental health professionals and faith leaders are trying to make sense of these experiences.

More importantly, I'll offer pastoral guidance for how to care for people who feel divided within themselves—those who live with torment, fragmentation, and fear. My hope is that this chapter will serve as a bridge between the fields of psychology and theology, offering insight to ministers, counselors, and lay leaders who want to walk wisely and compassionately in this space.

A gentle word of encouragement: don't be overwhelmed by the clinical language ahead. These reflections are not meant to be academic exercises. They are meant to equip people like you—pastors, prayer ministers, spiritual caregivers—to see the whole person and respond with both spiritual discernment and emotional intelligence.

What Is Dissociative Identity Disorder?

Dissociative Identity Disorder (DID)—once called Multiple Personality Disorder—is a complex and often misunderstood condition. At its core, DID is marked by a fractured sense of identity. People with DID experience two or more distinct identity states that take turns influencing how they think, feel, and act.[1] These shifts may be subtle or dramatic and are often accompanied by changes in memory, behavior, emotions, and even physical abilities.[2]

These identity states—or "alters"—may be perceived by the person as alternate versions of themselves, or, in some cultures, as external beings such as spirits or demons.[3] This is why the DSM-5 allows for the experience of possession to be part of DID's diagnostic profile in certain cultural contexts.

In addition to identity disruption, individuals often report significant memory gaps—forgetting everyday details, key personal information, or past trauma.[4] These memory losses go beyond normal forgetfulness and can interfere with work, relationships, and daily life.[5]

1. American Psychiatric Association, *Diagnostic and Statistical Manual*, 329.
2. American Psychiatric Association, *Diagnostic and Statistical Manual*, 329–30.
3. American Psychiatric Association, *Diagnostic and Statistical Manual*, 329–30. The following is a direct quote from the DSM. To meet the DSM-5 criteria for DID, the following must be present:
   A. Two or more distinct identity states causing a marked disruption in self and agency, which may include experiences of possession.
   B. Recurring memory gaps inconsistent with ordinary forgetting.
   C. Clinically significant distress or impairment in key areas of life.
   D. Not part of an accepted cultural or religious practice.
   E. Not caused by substance use or another medical
4. American Psychiatric Association, *Diagnostic and Statistical Manual*, 329–30.
5. American Psychiatric Association, *Diagnostic and Statistical Manual*, 329–30.

Importantly, DID is not diagnosed when these symptoms are the result of drug use, medical conditions, or accepted religious practices.[6] It arises from profound psychological distress, most often linked to severe and chronic trauma, especially during early childhood.[7]

Does DSM-5 Acknowledge Demons?

The DSM-5 does not pass judgment on whether demons or spirits exist; its language is descriptive rather than explanatory. Theological explanations, such as those offered by deliverance ministers, are considered outside the scope of clinical science. Nonetheless, the overlap between clinical and spiritual categories is difficult to ignore. The behaviors described under the possession form of DID—altered voice, changes in mannerism, memory gaps, a lack of agency, and apparent "takeover" by an unseen force—mirror the case studies of demonization described by countless pastors and exorcists.[8]

DID and Suicide

Complicating matters further is the severity of impairment experienced by those with DID. The DSM-5 notes that "over 70% of outpatients with dissociative identity disorder have attempted suicide, multiple attempts are common, and other self-injurious behavior is frequent."[9] Whether interpreted as psychological illness, spiritual bondage, or both, this is not a harmless or minor affliction.

Psychological or Spiritual?

For modern pastors, counselors, and clinicians, these data points raise critical questions. When someone presents with behaviors that appear to stem from an invasive spiritual force, is it solely an issue of mental health? Or could the ancient understanding of demonic possession still hold explanatory power?

6. American Psychiatric Association, *Diagnostic and Statistical Manual*, 329–30.
7. American Psychiatric Association, *Diagnostic and Statistical Manual*, 329–30.
8. American Psychiatric Association, *Diagnostic and Statistical Manual*, 330.
9. American Psychiatric Association, *Diagnostic and Statistical Manual*, 332.

In some cases, possession-form DID may result from trauma-based dissociation—a protective psychological mechanism that fractures identity to survive unbearable suffering. However, many pastors and exorcists describe encounters in which the behaviors seem to exceed what is typical of human psychology, especially when accompanied by paranormal activity.[10]

It is possible, perhaps even likely, that some cases of possession-form DID involve only internal psychological factors, while others may involve genuine spiritual affliction. A diagnosis of DID should never be casually dismissed, but neither should it preclude spiritual discernment—especially when symptoms persist despite comprehensive mental health treatment.

Multi-disciplinary Interpretation

As is often the case in complex human suffering, rigid dichotomies fail to serve those most in need. Deliverance ministers must be cautious not to label every identity disruption as demonic, just as mental health professionals must recognize that not all experiences can be reduced to trauma, neurochemistry, or personality structure. The integration of disciplines—clinical psychology, theology, and pastoral care—offers a more complete pathway toward freedom and healing.

In the end, possession-form DID challenges simplistic answers. It urges us to listen carefully, to discern wisely, and to remain open to the reality that human beings are both psychologically complex and spiritually vulnerable.

Alicia's Story: When Diagnosis Isn't Enough

Alicia had endured unimaginable trauma. She suffered abuse at the hands of her father during childhood and, later in life, became the victim of brutal sexual assault. As she struggled to process the violence committed against her, she began hearing voices and experiencing dissociative episodes. By the time she began therapy, her mind was fragmented, her emotions volatile, and her sense of self deeply fractured. Her therapist diagnosed her with DID—a label that initially brought a measure of comfort. At least now, she

10. Barry, "Qualitative Analysis," 55, 82, 98. This study focuses on seven individuals who experienced dissociative episodes and were treated with a form of exorcism. This chapter's later section on Dissociative Trance Disorder deals specifically with cases of dissociation where preternatural/paranormal signs are present.

had a name for the chaos, but while the diagnosis gave her a category, it didn't give her relief.

Alicia desperately wanted answers to her struggles. She turned to tarot readings, believing that God spoke to her through the cards. Her nights were filled with torment—vivid nightmares, unshakable dread, and household objects moving with no apparent cause. Whether her therapist dismissed these experiences as psychotic symptoms or chose to ignore them altogether remains unclear. Either way, Alicia was unraveling.

Desperate for help, Alicia's boyfriend reached out to a Christian friend who was studying psychology. He asked him to pray for her because he feared a demon may have been tormenting her. The friend and his wife sat down and visited with the two of them, trying to better understand what she was experiencing.

After that meeting, Alicia had a deeply distressing experience. A spiritual entity revealed itself to her, claiming the identity of a Norse god. Although it presented itself as an alter, she was able to see it walking around her house. She described it as a physical entity. Her boyfriend saw it as well. This wasn't simply a dissociative alter surfacing—it was something darker, more commanding, and malicious. They again reached out to the friend, asking him to come to their home and cast out the demon.

Rather than rushing into a spiritual battle, the friend engaged them in ongoing conversations which revealed the true depth of Alicia's entanglement. She admitted to actively practicing witchcraft and did not plan to stop. Even more concerning, she harbored intense hatred and adamantly refused to discuss the possibility of forgiveness.

Although the friend cared deeply and wanted to help, he also knew the spiritual stakes. He gently explained that without a willingness to renounce occult ties and begin the journey toward forgiveness, there was little he could do. She needed more than a diagnosis or a quick prayer. She needed real deliverance—and she needed to want that deliverance. Desperate to help but recognizing the necessity of leading Alicia into an encounter with Christ, he invited her and her boyfriend to attend a prayer meeting. Alicia showed inexplicable fear at the thought of entering the building for prayer, repeatedly stating she couldn't or "something bad would happen."

Alicia's therapist recognized the role that trauma had played in creating her dissociative symptoms. Her Christian friend recognized a spiritual power that was exacerbating her torment. Tragically, neither of them could help—because Alicia was not yet willing to choose healing. What she needed wasn't just therapy and it wasn't just prayer. She needed both. She needed an integrated, Spirit-empowered path to freedom. But more than that, she needed to let go of the darkness she was still embracing.

Was her DID diagnosis accurate? Perhaps. What's clear is this: The diagnosis did not account for the full reality of what she was experiencing. Because of that, her treatment fell short. Alicia's story reminds us that trauma, spiritual oppression, and human agency often intersect in complicated and heartbreaking ways.

As pastors, clinicians, and deliverance ministers, we must do better. We must create space for truth that holds complexity. We must always remember: Jesus is the only one who can bring full deliverance to body, soul, and spirit.

Dissociative Trance Disorder: A Closer Fit?

Most people reading this book are not clinicians, but many have encountered someone—or have themselves experienced—something that looks like spiritual possession. While the DSM-5 officially classifies these episodes as a subtype of DID, not everyone in the mental health field agrees with that decision. In fact, a growing number of professionals argue that possession experiences should be understood as their *own* category, separate from DID.[11] One leading candidate is Dissociative Trance Disorder (DTD).[12]

Though not formally recognized in the DSM-5, DTD has been widely documented across cultures and continents.[13] It usually presents as an altered state of consciousness in which a person claims to be taken over by an external force—like a spirit, deity, or supernatural being.[14] Unlike DID, which involves long-term identity fragmentation, DTD episodes are usually temporary and don't require someone to have multiple personalities or a long history of mental illness.[15]

In a landmark study, psychiatrist Emmanuel During and his colleagues reviewed 402 well-documented DTD cases from a 22-year period;

11. During et al., "Critical Review," 235–42.

12. During et al., "Critical Review," 241.

13. During et al., "Critical Review," 241.

14. During et al., "Critical Review," 238.

15. American Psychiatric Association, *Diagnostic and Statistical Manual*, 298; see also, During et al., "Critical Review," 238.

their research spanned dozens of cultures and several continents.[16] The findings were eye-opening:

- **69%** of the cases involved actual possession experiences (not just trance states).
- Only **3 out of 402** patients had any other diagnosed mental health disorder—starkly different from DID, where comorbidities are common.
- **56%** of patients reported seeing or hearing the spirit or entity controlling them.
- **80%** remained somewhat aware during their episodes (in contrast to the blackouts often seen in DID).
- The condition was observed globally—from Asia to Africa, and even in Catholic and Pentecostal settings in North America and Europe.[17]

The researchers concluded that DTD and DID may look similar on the surface, but underneath, they are fundamentally different.[18] DTD usually doesn't stem from early-life trauma, and many patients seem psychologically healthy outside of the possession episodes.[19] In that way, DTD more closely resembles the spiritual affliction that pastors and deliverance ministers often describe, rather than the identity fragmentation found in DID.

Here's how the researchers suggest we define DTD in possession cases:

> A temporary state in which a person's identity is replaced by another—described as a spirit, deity, or power—recognized by the person or those around them. This may include: (a) behavior, speech, or movements that appear to be controlled by that spirit, and/or (b) visual or auditory hallucinations related to the possessing entity.[20]

This definition strikes a balance—it respects the clinical need for clarity while also leaving room for the cultural and spiritual dimensions many people bring to their experience of affliction.

16. During et al., "Critical Review," 235.

17. During et al., "Critical Review," 235–39. "Comorbidity" is medical language for a co-occurring condition.

18. During et al., "Critical Review," 241.

19. American Psychiatric Association, *Diagnostic and Statistical Manual*, 298; see also, During et al., "Critical Review," 238.

20. During et al., "Critical Review," 238.

For both pastors and therapists, this matters. When someone comes forward claiming to be tormented or taken over, it's easy to either over-spiritualize or dismiss it as mental illness. DTD offers a more nuanced framework. It reminds us that some people suffer in ways that don't fit neatly into our categories—and that real healing might require both spiritual care and psychological insight.

Put simply: DTD bridges the gap. It helps pastors understand clinical language and invites clinicians to consider the spiritual framework their patients may be living in. Perhaps most importantly, it helps ensure that no one falls through the cracks simply because they don't fit our expectations.

Increasing Secularization

In recent decades, the field of psychiatry has grown more inclusive of cross-cultural perspectives, recognizing that people around the world interpret their mental and emotional struggles in very different ways. Yet even with this progress, there's been a noticeable drift—especially in the West—toward a purely secular understanding of psychological distress. For many, this shift has quietly edged out the spiritual categories that once played a central role in how we understood suffering.

Psychologist Alexander DiChiara documents the divorce of theology from secular psychology. He notes, "Exorcisms were plentiful in the sixteenth and seventeenth centuries, and this upsurge of cases created a great urgency to come up with answers. Throughout time, individuals looked to the Church . . . to help with this matter, but more recently, the tide has turned to science and psychology, to detrimental results."[21]

In an article published in *Psychiatric Times*, historian and psychologist Richard Noll offers a striking observation. Reflecting on the development of the *DSM-III-R*, he writes:

> The DSM-III-R Advisory Committee on Dissociative Disorders was conscious of the historical implications of the [Multiple Personality Disorder] MPD diagnosis, noting that MPD 'and its attenuated forms are, historically, the secularized descendants of the Judeo-Christian possession syndrome' (pg. 44).[22]

21. DiChiara, "Dissociation, Possession, Or Otherwise," 11.

22. Noll, "When Psychiatry Battled the Devil," 2. MPD is now known as DID.

In plain terms, Noll is saying that what we now call DID was once described—both culturally and clinically—as possession. And the architects of the DSM knew it. With a stroke of the pen, possession syndrome was reframed as a psychiatric diagnosis. Exorcists, once seen as spiritual specialists in these matters, were quietly replaced by therapists and psychiatrists. As Noll puts it, psychiatry began to "colonize the supernatural."[23]

This colonization wasn't necessarily driven by malice. Some professionals were likely trying to offer scientific, non-religious solutions to people suffering from symptoms that resembled possession. Others may have viewed the shift as a necessary move away from what they considered religious superstition. But here's the problem: just because you rename the land doesn't mean the original inhabitants pack up and leave.

For many individuals experiencing severe spiritual torment, the secular language of modern psychiatry doesn't tell their full story. While some cases of dissociation are best understood through psychological lenses, others seem to carry a spiritual weight that can't be explained away. In these instances, the soul feels *inhabited*—not just fragmented.

The growing tension between psychological explanations and spiritual realities is one reason why collaboration between pastors and mental health professionals is so essential. If we ignore the spiritual, we risk misdiagnosing those who may need deliverance. If we ignore the psychological, we risk retraumatizing those who need deep emotional healing.

The truth is, not every possession-type case is demonic, and not every trauma-induced episode can be fixed with therapy alone. We live in a world where both demons and disorders exist. The challenge—and the calling—is to discern which is which and respond with wisdom, compassion, and humility.

Possession Syndrome: Real Cases, Real Complexity

The term *possession syndrome* refers to a complex cluster of symptoms in which individuals exhibit behaviors traditionally associated with demonization—such as supernatural strength, disorganized identity, language anomalies, and altered states of consciousness—yet often receive psychiatric diagnoses rather than spiritual attention.[24] The following documented

23. Noll, "When Psychiatry Battled the Devil," 2.

24. World Health Organization, *The ICD-10*, 156.

cases from international clinical settings illustrate the profound need for an integrative, spiritually aware approach to care.

Speaking Arabic Without Learning It

Amin Gadit, a psychiatrist working in transcultural psychiatry, reports the case of a 21-year-old woman who presented with "extreme aggression," "extraordinary strength," and the spontaneous ability to speak Arabic, a language she had never studied.[25] These episodes, lasting "fifteen to twenty minutes" and occurring "at least three times" a week, were observed first-hand in the clinic.[26] Despite no history of trauma, no co-occurring psychiatric conditions, and no prior mental illness, she remained unresponsive to all pharmaceutical treatments.[27] Gadit noted the possibility of "possession by jinni" as a legitimate diagnostic category.[28]

Gadit's case meets several clinical criteria for DID but lacks the trauma typically required for diagnosis. It also aligns with "Possession Syndrome" as suggested by Gadit, though the ability to speak an unlearned language complicates purely psychiatric interpretations.[29] With medical options exhausted, spiritual intervention appeared not only warranted but necessary.

"Remove These Chains!"

Another case, documented by Collin Weintraub and Melissa P. Bui, describes a 53-year-old Southern Baptist man ("Mr. A") whose episodes included growling, speaking "in a demonic voice," engaging in self-injury, and exhibiting strength far beyond normal human capability.[30] After

25. Gadit, "Possession," 1. Her father acknowledged that she had learned to recite the "Holy Book" in Arabic but did not speak and understand Arabic. During her trance episodes, she was able to carry on full conversations in Arabic that mostly consisted of "cursing and blaming" and contained no recitations from their "Holy Book"; see also Saki and Ahmadi, "Spirit Possession, Mental Suffering, and Treatment," 567–92. Saki and Ahmadi's article mentions jinn possession on the next page. This footnote references a study from Iran that also addresses jinn possession. It is included here to expand the context of this phenomenon.

26. Gadit, "Possession," 1.

27. Gadit, "Possession," 1.

28. Gadit, "Possession," 1.

29. Gadit, "Possession," 1–2.

30. Weintraub and Bui, "'Remove These Chains,'" 661.

such episodes, he experienced "retrograde amnesia."[31] His wife reported that he also experienced disturbing olfactory hallucinations and vivid visual intrusions involving demonic imagery.[32] Despite ten inpatient psychiatric hospitalizations and consistent use of medication, he showed no improvement.[33]

During one clinical interview, Mr. A erupted mid-conversation and ripped off EEG leads, shouting "[Mr. A] isn't here anymore!" and began throwing objects with violent force, screaming "remove these chains!"[34] Strikingly, no brain activity indicating sleep, seizure, or dissociation was recorded before, during, or after the episode.[35] The authors concluded that "a spiritually focused modality of care should be considered."[36] For individuals like Mr. A, a pastoral or integrative intervention may prove vital—not only for healing but possibly for survival.

Cursed in an Unknown Language

Saad Asim Choudhry and colleagues describe a 28-year-old Pakistani woman who was admitted to the hospital after suffering "multiple burns"—inflicted by spiritual healers attempting to drive out what they believed to be demons.[37] Her symptoms included "aggressive behavior," physical violence, and shouting obscenities in Pushto, a language no one in her family spoke and which she had never studied.[38] She demonstrated extraordinary physical strength during these episodes and could not be subdued.[39]

Though diagnosed with DID and treated with olanzapine and therapy, her symptoms never fully resolved.[40] The researchers noted an overlap with

31. Weintraub and Bui, "Remove These Chains," 661.

32. Weintraub and Bui, "Remove These Chains," 661.

33. Weintraub and Bui, "Remove These Chains," 662.

34. Weintraub and Bui, "Remove These Chains," 661.

35. Weintraub and Bui, "Remove These Chains," 661.

36. Weintraub and Bui, "Remove These Chains," 662.

37. Choudhry et al., "Case of Possession Syndrome," 543.

38. Choudhry et al., "Case of Possession Syndrome," 543.

39. Choudhry et al., "Case of Possession Syndrome," 543.

40. Choudhry et al., "Case of Possession Syndrome," 543. This study's assertion that the patient had "no remission" leads one to conclude that there was never a full resolution of symptoms. Although a decrease in symptoms was observed within the study, it is reasonable to conclude the possibility that adding a spiritually focused treatment to her plan would have been worth considering, especially given the study's acknowledgement

psychosis but could not identify a definitive syndrome.[41] Again, the spiritual and cultural dimensions of her condition went largely unaddressed. While her trauma was physical rather than psychological, her affliction aligned closely with what others have called possession syndrome.

Integrative Models and Global Implications

A study conducted in Uganda examined more than 100 individuals diagnosed with possession syndrome using a culturally integrative approach.[42] Though the researchers identified strong links between trauma and current distress, they found that 99 percent of participants reported significant improvement—and more than half reported complete healing—after undergoing a culturally sanctioned exorcism, without direct therapeutic engagement with their trauma.[43] These findings challenge many assumptions in Western psychiatry about the nature of healing.

Psychotherapist Michael Sersch reflects on studies like these, observing that "exorcism may prove more effective than conventional treatments for conditions like DID and schizophrenia among patients culturally conditioned to believe in it."[44] In communities where spiritual explanations hold sway, interventions that respect those frameworks often lead to better outcomes than biomedical approaches alone.

Scholars Khan and Sahni affirm the need for collaborative engagement between theological and medical communities. They acknowledge:

> Drug resistant cases of Possession Syndrome have been cured by exorcism, as well as people have died in the hands of exorcists for want of medical attention. . . . The concept of possession should be observed as a disease condition and a harmonizing approach advocated. Theological perspective can be amalgamated with current scientific theory and practice, thereby complementing existing concepts. Possession syndrome and exorcism may be incorporated into some paradigm of illness.[45]

---

that she was able to speak languages she had not learned and displayed extraordinary strength, features that are not fully explained by a purely psychiatric disorder but that are consistent with a diagnosis of spirit possession.

41. Choudhry et al., "Case of Possession Syndrome," 544.

42. Van Duijl et al., "Dissociative Symptoms and Reported Trauma," 380.

43. Van Duijl et al., "Dissociative Symptoms and Reported Trauma," 395.

44. Sersch, *Demons on the Couch,* 130–38.

45. Khan and Sahni, "Possession Syndrome at High Altitude," 255.

This call for harmonization reflects a growing awareness: spiritual problems and psychological disorders are not mutually exclusive. The most effective solutions will likely involve partnership, humility, and a shared desire for the person's total well-being.

While pastors and clinicians may look through distinct lenses, the distinctions between spiritual and psychological realities are often far blurrier than either discipline prefers to admit. The pressing need is for compassionate leaders on both sides of the aisle to acknowledge this complexity, listen to each other, and minister—together—to those whose pain defies simple categorization.

Pastoral vs. Clinical Interpretation

The church must avoid two extremes:

1. **Over-spiritualizing psychological pain** (treating every alter or trauma response as a demon)
2. **Over-pathologizing spiritual experiences** (dismissing genuine cases of demonization as mental illness)[46]

Both the clinical and pastoral communities have insights to offer. When they collaborate, healing becomes possible.

Beyond Labels, Toward Liberation

Ministering to those who are tormented—whether by psychological fragmentation, spiritual darkness, or both—is sacred work. This chapter has sought to clarify the clinical language surrounding dissociative disorders while honoring the very real spiritual dynamics at play. For too long, these two spheres—mental health and deliverance—have stood at odds, each suspicious of the other's claims. But those caught in the crossfire don't need a debate. They need discernment. They need healing.

It is not always easy to distinguish between a divided soul and a tormented one. Sometimes the lines blur. Sometimes they don't exist at all. Still, faith leaders should never shy away from complexity. Instead, we are

46. DiChiara, "Dissociation, Possession, or Otherwise," 5. DiChiara writes, "The pathologizing of a person's experience into such a disorder has detrimental effects on the person and alienates them further."

invited to sit with people in their pain, to listen carefully, to pray boldly, and to walk humbly alongside trained professionals when needed.

The reality is this: trauma shatters people, and sin invites darkness. Still, Jesus Christ is more than capable of restoring wholeness—whether through truth, through therapy, through exorcism, or through all three. As you move into the next chapter on inner healing, carry with you the conviction that no soul is too broken, no wound too deep, and no darkness too strong for the light of Christ to reach. Let us be ministers who do not reduce people to diagnoses or demons, but who see them as image-bearers in need of both liberation and restoration.

In the end, whether we are confronting demons or dissociative parts, our calling remains the same: to partner with the Holy Spirit in the healing work of Jesus—restoring the shattered, reclaiming the oppressed, and walking alongside the wounded until they are whole again.

Questions to Discuss

1. When a person's behavior includes both psychological symptoms (e.g., identity fragmentation) and apparent spiritual phenomena (e.g., unlearned languages, supernatural strength), how should ministers and mental health professionals work together to respond?
2. How does Alicia's story illustrate the limits of a purely clinical diagnosis or a purely spiritual approach?
3. What dangers exist in over-spiritualizing trauma-related disorders, and what dangers exist in over-pathologizing spiritual experiences?
4. Why is Dissociative Trance Disorder (DTD) an important concept for pastors and clinicians to understand, and how might it help bridge the gap between spiritual and psychological interpretations of possession-like symptoms?
5. What practical safeguards can be put in place in your ministry or church to ensure that people presenting with possible dissociation or possession are treated with both compassion and discernment?

Chapter 9

Healing the Divided Soul

We live in a divided world, but long before the culture fractured, people were already walking around fractured from within. Some carry wounds from childhood that split their sense of self. Others bear years of trauma buried so deep they can't remember what happened. They just know that they don't feel whole. Many believers live double lives—publicly strong, privately tormented. Some of the people who walk into our churches smiling every Sunday are silently screaming on the inside.

This is the reality of soul fragmentation.

In the world of psychology, it is called *dissociation*. In the spiritual world, we often see it as a point of entry for demonic torment. In the life of the church, it's one of the most misunderstood and under-discussed aspects of deliverance ministry.

Here's the good news: Jesus heals the divided soul. He doesn't just cast demons out. He gathers the pieces of our identity and makes us whole again.

A Fractured Soul in a Fallen World

Fragmentation is not a spiritual failure. It's a survival strategy. When children endure prolonged trauma—abuse, neglect, or terror—the mind and soul find a way to cope by separating painful memories from conscious awareness. In extreme cases this can develop into dissociative identity disorder, which was discussed in the previous chapter.

In some people, these fragmented parts of the soul become so distinct they feel like different personalities. In others, they manifest as emotional swings, memory lapses, or behavioral contradictions.

Psychologist Stephen Diamond has written extensively about individuals overtaken by powerful emotions or internal forces.[1] Drawing on the work of his mentor, Rollo May, Diamond reclaims the ancient Greek idea of the *daimon*—a word from which we derive the modern term "demon." In their usage, however, the term does not refer to a supernatural being, but to the capacity of natural human drives to overtake and dominate the self. May defines the daimonic as "any natural function which has the power to take over the whole person. Sex and eros, anger and rage, and the craving for power are examples. . . When this power goes awry, and one element usurps control over the total personality, we have 'daimon possession.'"[2]

This view highlights the sobering reality that a person may appear to be under demonic control when, in fact, they are overpowered by their own emotional drives. Rage, fear, sexual desire, trauma, and rejection can create internal storms so intense that rational thought is overridden. While this is not possession in the biblical sense, it bears a striking resemblance to it in experience and manifestation.

Diamond describes such moments with startling intensity:

> Patients in this profoundest state of insanity or madness do not simply talk about believing themselves to be possessed: they scream it, bellow it, act it out, experience it in the white-hot core of their being, in all its holy terror and intensity. They are wholly and deliriously clutched in the gut-wrenching grips of the daimonic.[3]

What is operating in these moments is not an external demon but an unintegrated and overwhelming force from within the human psyche.

T. Craig Isaacs, both a psychologist and an Anglican priest with experience in exorcism, builds on this understanding while holding fast to biblical theology. In *Revelations and Possessions*, Isaacs affirms the reality of demonic influence but introduces the idea of soul fragmentation as a parallel—and sometimes overlapping—phenomenon.[4] He conceptualizes

1. Diamond, *Anger, Madness, and the Daimonic.*
2. May, *Love and Will*, 121.
3. Diamond, *Anger, Madness, and the Daimonic*, Kindle Loc 2659.
4. Isaacs, *Revelations and Possessions*, 29–31.

the human soul as a "committee" made up of all the significant experiences, traumas, relationships, and memories that have shaped a person.[5] These internal voices—whether drawn from Adverse Childhood Experiences (ACES), broken attachments, or religious encounters—can each carry their own emotional charge, including fear, shame, anger, rejection, or a drive for self-preservation.

When the soul becomes fractured or disintegrated, one or more elements of this inner committee may dominate the rest. Isaacs describes this as a form of internal possession—not by a demon, but by a part of the self that has broken away and seized control.[6] While this may look like classic possession, its roots are psychological rather than spiritual. Isaacs is careful to acknowledge that demonic influence can still be present in such cases but clarifies that this is not the same as demonic possession.[7] In these situations, deliverance ministry must be accompanied by emotional healing and soul integration. Casting out a demon will not bring peace if the invading force is not "wholly other" but rather a dissociated part of the self.[8]

This perspective helps explain why some deliverance sessions appear to fail: the torment is real, but its source is internal. Only when the fragmented soul is tended to through forgiveness, integration, and healing can lasting peace be restored. Nonetheless, breaking free from this kind of bondage may require a significant battle. Diamond writes, "No matter how 'possessed' or 'pushed' or 'driven' we may be. . .there is always potentially some degree of freedom—minuscule as it might seem—to consciously choose one's personal response or one's attitude toward these awesome powers."[9]

Now, what if spiritual torment is added into the mix? A wounded part of the soul, especially one isolated and forgotten, can become vulnerable to spiritual intrusion. A demon may attach itself to that part, creating intense symptoms: self-harm, tormenting thoughts, suicidal urges, or even alternate voices and body movements.

This doesn't mean the person is "crazy." It means they were wounded—and need both spiritual liberation and psychological integration.

5. Isaacs, *Revelations and Possessions*, 20–30, 89–93.

6. Isaacs, *Revelations and Possessions*, 24–31, 65–69; see also, Isaacs, *In Bondage to Evil*, 157.

7. Isaacs, *Revelations and Possessions*, 143–47.

8. Isaacs, *Revelations and Possessions*, chap 3 and 4 and pg. 145–46; see also, Isaacs, *In Bondage to Evil*, 161.

9. Diamond, *Anger, Madness, and the Daimonic*, chap 4.

Luke's Story: The Limits of One-Time Deliverance

While language like "soul possession" may not have been part of my vocabulary at the time, I encountered something remarkably similar years ago—except in this case, there was also a definite demonic element.

I was standing beside one of my mentors, Abel Ramsundar, as he led a prayer service. Abel looked out at the crowd and called a young man named Luke forward. At the time, I had no idea that Luke had made up his mind that this would be his last time attending church. He was angry—visibly, deeply, and spiritually angry. The moment he stepped forward, I silently thanked God that someone else would be the one to pray for him. To my horror, Abel turned, looked straight at me, and said, "Robbie, pray for him." Without another word, he walked off.

I hesitated for a moment, but I placed my hand on Luke's shoulder and began to pray. As soon as I touched him, he collapsed to the floor. At first, it seemed like a breakthrough. I heard him weeping, crying out to God with deep anguish, saying, "I don't want to be angry anymore. Please God, take away this anger." My heart broke. I knelt beside him and prayed with compassion, quietly speaking, "In the Name of Jesus Christ, you spirit of anger, come out of him."

What happened next was unlike anything I'd ever experienced. Luke shifted—suddenly, violently—and launched into a blind rage. He grabbed me with one hand and threw me across the sanctuary. Before my body had fully hit the ground, he was already on top of me, eyes rolled back, veins bulging, trying to wrap his hands around my throat. His strength was overwhelming. I fought to keep his grip from closing in, and amid the chaos, I found just enough clarity to speak again: "In the Name of Jesus, stop. Get off me!"

He fell as though struck by a force greater than both of us. The anger vanished. The violent rage gave way to brokenness, and Luke now lay there pleading with God for salvation and healing. It felt like a spiritual victory. It was a moment I'll never forget.

Over time, however, I came to see it differently. At that stage in my life, I wrongly believed that deliverance alone was enough. The demon had left; surely that was the end of it, but it wasn't. Luke continued to struggle. In hindsight, it was clear: While there was undeniable demonic torment, there were also layers of psychological and emotional wounds that had not been addressed. Luke needed something more than just one encounter. He needed sustained pastoral care, clinical support, and ongoing healing. He was no longer demonized, but his soul was still fragmented; he was broken. I didn't have the language or the understanding to see it at the time, but my ignorance left him vulnerable.

I have no doubt that the Name of Jesus saved Luke's life that night. Still, freedom is not always instantaneous—it is often a process. Luke needed more than a one-time deliverance; he needed discipleship, healing, and integration.

The Need for Both: Liberation and Integration

Historically, the church has excelled in confronting demons, but it has struggled to understand emotional bondage and dissociation. On the other hand, therapists often understand trauma but lack the spiritual discernment or understanding to address demonic influence. The solution is not to pick sides. It's to bring them together.

Liberation is the removal of demonic spirits through prayer, repentance, and the authority of Jesus. **Integration** is the restoration and realignment of fractured parts of the soul through inner healing, therapy, and community support.

When we combine the two, we don't just remove the torment—we restore the person. This approach doesn't abandon biblical theology—it fulfills it. Jesus said he came to "proclaim liberty to the captives and recovery of sight to the blind, to set at liberty those who are oppressed. . ." (Luke 4:18).

That includes every part of us—body, soul, and spirit.

Diamond offers profound insight into the necessity of helping individuals process traumatic experiences in a healthy and redemptive way. Reflecting on the enduring impact of childhood wounds, he writes:

> Some childhood wounding or trauma is inevitable in this imperfect world of ours. And such fateful psychic damage becomes our daimon—part of our destiny—forming our character and more or less informing our future actions. In adulthood, emotional laceration may be recognized, made conscious, placed in a wider perspective and, sometimes, even healed. But 'healing' does not mean forgetting, for to become conscious is to remember and to know. Healing entails the mature acceptance of the traumatic facts of one's emotional mortification, the causes and the consequences, as well as a resolute willingness to swallow the following bitter pill: We cannot change the past nor undo the wound. Nor can we realistically hope as adults to now magically receive that which, in so many cases, brought about the original wounding by dint

> of its absence during infancy, childhood or adolescence. We can, nonetheless, allow ourselves to feel our rage and grief over this irretrievable loss. We have the freedom and power to determine our attitude toward the past. We may even—with some good fortune, time and grace—find within ourselves the capacity to forgive those who we feel inflicted our agonizing injuries.[10]

Diamond's insistence that traumatized individuals be allowed "to feel our rage and grief over this irretrievable loss" offers a critical challenge to deliverance and discipleship models alike. It reminds us that freedom from torment is not simply about driving out darkness; it is also about holding space for sorrow and giving voice to pain. Pastors and mental health professionals alike can create safe environments where individuals are encouraged to remember, reflect, and release. When spiritual leaders create space for honest grief and integrate prayer, Scripture, and forgiveness into the healing journey, the soul begins to mend. Healing is not found in denying our wounds but in naming them, processing them, and discovering, by grace, that we are not defined by them.

What This Looks Like in Ministry

In practical ministry, here's what healing a divided soul might involve:

1. Identifying Parts

If someone does not know what caused the distress they are experiencing, it can be helpful to begin by asking, "When did this start?" They may respond with something like, "I have felt this way ever since I was twelve years old." *When* a struggle began is often the key to identifying *what* caused it. After asking when it started, ask, "What else happened around that time in life that stands out as significant?" The answer is often quite telling. Perhaps it was a death in the family or an experience of abuse. In one case, a woman had been in an auto accident when she was young and that was the starting point for her struggle with extreme fear. This is not an exact science, but the process of discovery can be powerful.

A person may say, "Part of me wants to trust God, but part of me feels afraid." Don't dismiss that language. It may indicate a soul part—often a young version of the person stuck in trauma. Gently ask, "Can you tell me

10. Diamond, *Anger, Madness, and the Daimonic*, chap 8.

more about that part of you that feels afraid?" Allow the Holy Spirit to bring that part into the light—not to shame it, but to comfort it.

2. Inviting Jesus In

Once the part is present, invite Jesus into the memory, the pain, or the place where that part is stuck. This is not imagination—it's encounter. Jesus meets us in the depths of our story and brings peace. I often pray something like this with people, "Heavenly Father, I am asking you to bring healing by revealing your presence within those moments when it felt like you were absent."

Often, when Jesus enters that space, the part of the soul begins to integrate. It no longer has to hide or protect itself. It can rest.

3. Discerning Spiritual Intrusion

Some soul parts may be guarded by a demonic presence—especially if the person was abused, abandoned, or made inner vows like "I'll never trust anyone again." These vows can give demons ground to oppress that part.

With discernment and compassion, speak to the spirit—not the person. Command it to leave in Jesus's name, but always do so in the context of healing, not confrontation alone.

4. Reclaiming Wholeness

As parts begin to integrate and spirits are cast out, the person starts to experience peace, clarity, and emotional freedom. Their mind feels quieter. Their emotions stabilize. Their identity becomes clearer. They often say something like, "I feel lighter." This is deliverance as discipleship. It takes time, safety, and the presence of Jesus.

Therapeutic Exorcism: A Collaborative Model

A growing number of Christian counselors and deliverance ministers are beginning to practice a form of "therapeutic exorcism."[11] This isn't about dramatic showdowns. It's a gentle, trauma-informed process where:

11. Dennis Bull, whose research is evaluated in chapter 11, is one author who uses this term.

- The therapist or minister helps the person identify soul parts.
- The parts are invited into connection with Jesus.
- Any demonic attachments are renounced and cast out.
- The person is supported in processing memories and integrating healing over time.

This model reflects the ministry of Jesus, who never rushed healing—but always restored fully. It also protects both the minister and the person. Deliverance isn't forced, and integration isn't rushed. Every step is covered in prayer and discernment.

James's Story: The Possession No One Expected

I wish I had understood the importance of a therapeutic approach before meeting James. James had always struggled with darkness just beneath the surface. From his earliest memories, there were moments that didn't quite fit into a normal childhood. One night, while still in primary school, he saw a man standing in the doorway of his bedroom. At first, he thought it was one of his parents. The figure looked familiar—almost like family—but it didn't belong there. When he blinked, it vanished.

In the years that followed, James saw more dark figures—some hovering above him with glowing red eyes. He also began to battle deep internal conflicts: bursts of rage, intrusive thoughts of violence, and overwhelming self-hatred. He punched himself, slapped himself, and called himself names. All the while, he remained outwardly composed—a kind, empathetic young man.

"It felt like warring factions inside my brain. I never heard voices, but there were *nudges*—to hurt myself, to look into harmful things, even to hurt others. I never acted on them, but they were always there. I didn't know anything was wrong, because it had always been that way."

James described it as living with a spiritual limp—like an old scar that still itches. Though he was now an adult, the roots of his torment stretched all the way back into his childhood. The pain had shape, history, and intelligence.

A Deliverance That Wasn't Planned

When I first met James, he was well-mannered and thoughtful, though clearly wrestling with anger and struggling with sinful patterns and relational strain. He hadn't come to us for prayer. In fact, we were ministering to his girlfriend that night—a session focused on past trauma and potential spiritual bondage.

James remembers thinking:

"Wow, I'm so glad this isn't me."

But God had other plans.

Because of their sexual relationship, we felt it was wise to also pray for James—to close any spiritual doors that may have been opened. He agreed, fully expecting it to be a routine moment of intercession. Instead, he blacked out.

The Dark World Behind His Eyes

What followed was not just emotional—it was spiritual and deeply supernatural. James later described it:

"I awoke in a dark world filled with vast nothingness. There was a door, and a little girl. Behind her stood a large Native American with an axe in his head. I grew up on tribal land and am a member of the Cherokee Nation. I knew who he was. My grandfather has a grave marker for a tribal elder on his property. This felt like him."

James was terrified of the man and began praying. The man disappeared. But then, the little girl reappeared.

"She was thin, pale, petite. . . Her hair was black as night. She was calm at first. But then her jaw distended unnaturally, and she screamed. Her face distorted. That's when she revealed herself."

In the physical world, James's body was manifesting. He threw furniture, cursed those around him, and threatened people's lives. A chair had been knocked over. Furniture was shifted. No one present doubted what was happening.

James had no memory of this. "It was like being drunk and suddenly becoming sober again. . .like a headache you've had for years just vanishing. Everything was quiet. Peaceful."

The Aftermath and the Lessons Learned

The next few days were wonderful for James. The torment was gone. The internal rage was silenced. He described it as a soul-level detox—like a spa for the spirit. He felt light. Free.

Still, James's story also reveals the limitations of well-meaning but inexperienced deliverance. As the one leading the session, I must admit that I was unprepared. When James began manifesting, I allowed myself to become frightened. I raised my voice and lost composure. I didn't lead him gently or follow up with aftercare. I simply wasn't mature enough to know better.

In God's mercy, James found freedom, but the trauma of the experience was real. In the years that followed, he struggled again—with depression, suicidal ideation, and isolation. Thankfully, James eventually found healing. He married. He became a father, and he found peace with God and rediscovered stability. I know now that if I had been better equipped, his recovery could have started much sooner. I have repented of my errors and, to be fully transparent, they are part of the inspiration behind this book.

What We Must Learn

The intelligence and violence of what manifested through James were undeniable. The signs had been there for years: childhood visions, self-directed violence, intrusive thoughts of harming others, and spiritual oppression masquerading as mood. They didn't fully surface until that moment of prayer, but that didn't make them any less real.

James's story reminds us that not all torment is mental illness, but it also reminds us that deliverance must be handled with care. Aggression from the minister doesn't drive out demons—Christ's authority does. Emotion doesn't win the battle—discernment does. Freedom is not just about the moment; it's about the journey that follows.

Why This Matters for the Church

The church must become a sanctuary for the shattered. Not every case of fragmentation will involve demons, but many will. Not every case of deliverance needs therapy, but some do. We must become people who understand the complexity of the soul without sacrificing the simplicity of the gospel.

Jesus doesn't flinch at our fractures. He doesn't reject our wounded parts. He calls us to wholeness—and he walks with us until we get there.

We need pastors who are trauma-informed. We need counselors who are Spirit-filled. We need communities where the broken can be rebuilt without shame. When integration and liberation work together, the result is powerful: not just freedom from torment, but the *recovery of self.*

Whole and Free

Deliverance is not just the casting out of darkness—it is the calling back of the self. For those who live fragmented by trauma, shame, or spiritual invasion, healing isn't merely about removal. It's about *reunion*. It's about Jesus gathering the broken pieces and saying, "You are mine."

In this chapter, we've seen that soul fragmentation is real: clinically, spiritually, and pastorally. We've also seen that it's not the end of the story. Whether the divisions within a person come from trauma or demonic torment (or both), the path to healing remains the same: truth, compassion, and the presence of Christ.

Integration is not a modern alternative to deliverance—it is its completion. For when Jesus sets a person free, he doesn't stop at eviction. He moves in. He restores the house. He puts the family photo back on the wall.

To minister in this space is sacred work. It requires discernment, patience, and a refusal to settle for surface-level victories. If we are willing to walk with the fractured—to name the parts, to invite Jesus in, to confront what must go, and to reclaim what has been lost—then we will see people not only delivered but made whole.

Questions to Discuss

1. In what ways does understanding soul fragmentation change how we approach deliverance ministry?
2. Luke's and James's stories both reveal the limits of a one-time deliverance. What does this teach us about the importance of aftercare and discipleship?

3. T. Craig Isaacs describes fragmentation as an "internal possession" by a part of the self. How does this challenge the idea that all manifestations of control are caused by demons?
4. Why is it important for pastors to be trauma-informed and for counselors to be Spirit-filled when ministering to fragmented souls?
5. The chapter ends with the statement that "integration is not a modern alternative to deliverance—it is its completion." How can churches practically embody this principle in their ministries?

Chapter 10

Diagnosing Demonization

IN 1973, WILLIAM PETER Blatty's film *The Exorcist* stunned moviegoers and ignited a cultural firestorm around the topic of demonic possession.[1] Loosely inspired by the real-life exorcism of a teenage boy under the care of Jesuit priest William S. Bowdern, Blatty's fictional account introduced the world to a deeply disturbing image: a young girl, possessed and tormented by a violent spirit.[2] Though exaggerated for effect, the film left a lasting impression. In the decades since its release, *The Exorcist* has become the definitive visual reference point for possession, both sparking public curiosity and shaping the modern imagination with terrifying images of supernatural control.

In many ways, this cinematic depiction helped raise awareness that spiritual torment exists—and that there is a need for deliverance.[3] But while it succeeded in stirring cultural interest, it also entrenched false assumptions about what demonization really looks like. As demonic themes have flourished in media—from horror films to docuseries and paranormal investigations—the result has been a surge in both fascination and misinformation.[4]

1. Allen, *Possessed*, x.

2. Allen, *Possessed*, xi–xii.

3. Cuneo, *American Exorcism*, 5–13.

4. Chavez, "Modern Practice, Archaic Ritual," 5, 22. While Cuneo's research used data leading up to 1998, Chavez notes on page 5 (referenced above) that from 1998 forward there have been "more than thirty exorcism films."

Pastors today are often approached by people whose expectations about spiritual warfare have been shaped more by Hollywood than by Scripture.

The decision of many deliverance ministers and pastoral leaders to use the term demonized rather than possessed is, in part, an effort to distance themselves from this confusion.[5] This distinction is not just semantic; it reflects a more nuanced understanding that is both biblical and pastoral. Unlike cinematic possession, which is often depicted as total, uncontrollable domination, demonization exists on a spectrum—ranging from subtle harassment to profound oppression, and in rare cases, full-blown control. Most cases are far less dramatic than what's shown on screen, yet the psychological and spiritual toll is very real.

This chapter addresses one of the most crucial and difficult questions in deliverance ministry: How do we diagnose demonization? What signs indicate the presence of an unclean spirit, and how do we differentiate between spiritual torment, psychological illness, and trauma? Drawing from biblical insight, clinical observation, and pastoral experience, this chapter offers a framework for recognizing the signs of demonization—so that freedom can be pursued with both discernment and compassion.[6]

The Importance of Discernment Over Assumption

People often associate dramatic behaviors—like screaming, convulsing, or speaking in strange voices—with demonic activity. While these can be signs, they are not definitive on their own. Such responses can also occur in cases of trauma, mental illness, or neurological dysfunction.

5. Willis, "Liberation and Integration," 89, 159, 251–53; see also, Heiser, *Demons*, 254. As I noted on pages 252–53 regarding theological and pastoral perspectives, "Most popular-level writing on this subject, as well as a significant amount of scholarly literature, transliterates the [Greek] word "*daimonizomai*" to create the word "demonized." Demonization is used to describe the spectrum of demonic attacks that are depicted in the New Testament and attested to by deliverance ministers and exorcists today." However, as noted on page 89, "Whereas many exorcists prefer the term "demonized" because it can refer to a spectrum of demonic activity, clinicians use the word "possession" to denote a psychological syndrome in which a person's identity appears to be replaced by an ego-alien entity. Many, though not all, mental health professionals see this as a purely psychological phenomenon."

6. This chapter intentionally reiterates information shared in previous chapters to create a cohesive picture of how to diagnose demonization.

The Apostle Paul reminded the church, "The natural man does not receive the things of the Spirit of God . . . because they are spiritually discerned" (1 Cor 2:14). That principle applies here. We must not rely solely on external observations. We need the gifts of the Spirit, especially the discerning of spirits, as well as pastoral training and clinical humility.

Understanding the Spectrum of Influence

Not all demonic activity is the same. Some attacks are subtle. Others are severe. Throughout this book, we have reviewed research by ministry leaders like Pablo Bottari, and Francis MacNutt, along with Psychiatrists like Richard Gallagher and M. Scott Peck, and clinical psychologists like T. Craig Isaacs and Alyson Barry, all who describe a spectrum of demonic influence.

The terminology may differ, but most agree that possession, in its truest form, is relatively rare—and it typically involves a surrender of the will to demonic control. Oppression, on the other hand, is far more common. It includes harassment, torment, or influence without full loss of control.

When discerning where someone is on this spectrum, the pastoral question is not simply, *"Is this person possessed?"* but rather, *"To what degree has the enemy gained access to this person's life—and how can they be made free?"*

Three Major Doorways to Demonization

In chapter 6, we identified three primary doorways through which demonic influence enters a person's life. Allow me to briefly recap them:

1. **Personal Sin**

   Habitual, unrepented sin opens the soul to darkness. Sin weakens moral clarity, damages the will, and invites deception. Eventually, spiritual sickness takes root. If unchecked, it can result in a driven, demonized condition.[7]

2. **Trauma**

   Deep wounding, especially in childhood, creates fragmentation and disintegration in the soul.[8] Unclean spirits prey on the vulnerable.

7. Isaacs, *In Bondage to Evil*, 169; see also, Isaacs, *Revelations and Possessions*, 112; see also, Lozano, *Unbound*, 40; see also, Ripperger, *Dominion*, 438–39.

8. Diamond, *Anger, Madness, and the Daimonic*, chap 8; see also, McChesney, *Soul*

Where trauma leaves people isolated and emotionally unguarded, demonic torment can often follow.[9]

3. **Occult Involvement**

   In addition to direct involvement, excessive curiosity and investigation of the occult has been reported to open doors in some cases.[10] While not everyone who dabbles in the occult becomes demonized, those who do often suffer the most severe cases.[11]

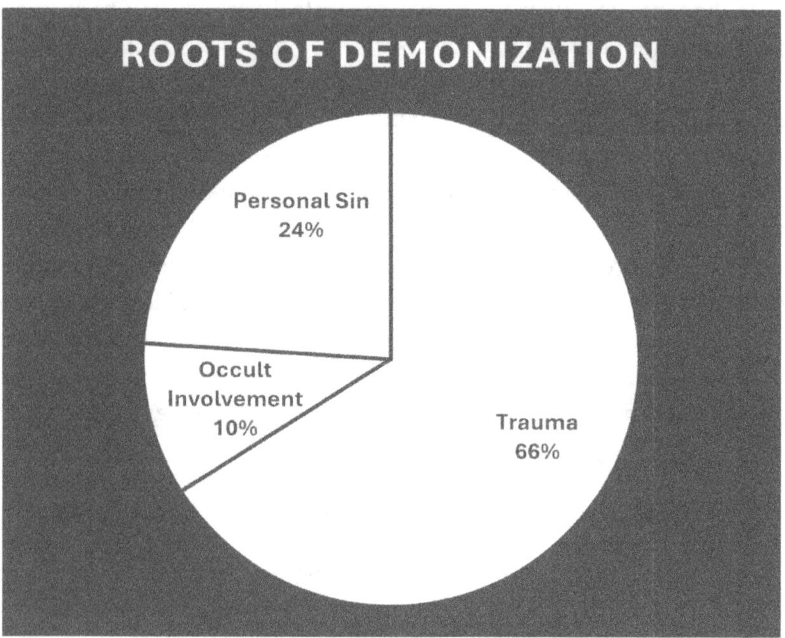

Pastors must listen carefully to a person's story, looking for these themes—not to judge, but to discern the path to healing. After all, it's hard to treat what you don't really understand. If people's distress began through traumatic experiences, wise pastors will approach things differently than if it is rooted in compulsive sin or occult rituals.

Also Keeps the Score.

9. MacNutt, *Deliverance*, 93.

10. Montgomery, *Demon Possession*, 268–69.

11. MacNutt, *Deliverance from Evil Spirits*, 91; see also, Willis, "Liberation and Integration," 255. The graphic at the top of this page represents the approximate percentages of people in the United States who become demonized through each of these three pathways according to my research.

Criteria for Possession—When Discernment Confirms the Extreme

There is no substitute for spiritual discernment. The voice and gifts of the Holy Spirit are indispensable when it comes to deliverance and healing. With that said, in extreme cases of demonization, there should be objective signs that validate the presence of the demonic. T. Craig Isaacs, a Christian psychotherapist and exorcist, developed a diagnostic framework for what he calls the "possessive states disorder." His work outlines three primary indicators of genuine possession cases:

A. The experience of being controlled by someone or something other than oneself, with subsequent loss of control in at least one of four areas:
   - Thinking
   - Anger or profanity
   - Impulsivity
   - Physical functioning

B. A fluctuating sense of self—periods of emptiness alternating with periods of inflation. These shifts aren't triggered by external circumstances but reflect an internal battle for control.

C. One or more of the following observable signs:
   - Hearing coherent voices that seem external
   - Seeing dark figures or apparitions
   - Trance-like states or the presence of multiple personalities
   - Drastic voice or language changes
   - Intense negative reactions to prayer or sacred objects
   - Paranormal manifestations (e.g., levitation, telepathy, unexplainable strength)[12]

12. Isaacs, *In Bondage to Evil*, 169, 211–12. The three-part diagnostic model is quoted directly from this source. Isaacs also provides additional characteristics to look for when A, B, and C are all present. The following additional characteristics are directly quoted from the same pages noted above:

The patient experiences a vision, voice, or feeling as coming from outside of him- or herself, attributed to a wholly other. The important aspect here is that the event is a spontaneous, immediate experience, rather than a subsequent interpretation of an event

Isaacs explains that these symptoms should not be confused with mere emotional distress. They indicate a deeper presence—an intelligent, uninvited entity influencing or controlling the person from within.[13]

The Value of Objective Signs

I am a firm believer in spiritual discernment and in following the Holy Spirit's guidance. There is no substitute for the supernatural when it comes to identifying demons and casting them out. Nonetheless, none of us are immune to the pitfall of bias and assumption. Even mature individuals tend to interpret situations through the lens of their own experience, education, and training. These lenses can aid us in proper discernment, but in some circumstances, they may also deceive us.

What is the solution? First, we should remember that when Jesus sent his disciples out with authority over unclean spirits, he sent them in pairs of two (Mark 6:7). There is always value in getting someone else's perspective and discernment. Second, identifying and documenting objective signs of demonic activity is a powerful deterrent against making assumptions.

The Catholic tradition, as preserved in the *Rituale Romanum*, identifies three clear signs that strongly indicate possession:

1. The ability to speak or understand unknown languages.
2. Knowledge of hidden or future events.
3. Strength or abilities beyond natural capacity.[14]

---

as having come from the wholly other.

The experience is numinous.

The presence of numinous fear or awe.

There is an unusual clarity to the experience; a clarity marked by the gaining of a cognizance that is instantaneous rather than gradual (like the awareness gained when listening to another person speaking rather than the knowledge gained by means of reasoning through a personal thought). Clarity is also exhibited in the establishment of the experience in long-lasting memory.

When a visual image is involved, there is some form of luminosity involved, whether of beautiful light or of shadowy darkness.

13. Isaacs, *In Bondage to Evil*, 169.

14. Weller, *Roman Ritual*, Part XIII: Exorcism, chap 1; see also, Bourguignon, "Hallucination and Trance," 184, 187; see also, Bourguignon, *Possession*; Bhavsar et al., "Dissociative Trance and Spirit Possession," 551–59; see also, Vaughan, *Phenomenal Phenomena*. Anthropologist Erika Bourguignon's global study on dissociation and altered states of consciousness finds that among 488 researched societies, possession states exist

Dr. Richard Gallagher is a board-certified psychiatrist who earned his medical degree at Yale University and is widely considered the world's leading medical expert on possession states. He adds additional indicators like levitation, trance states, and clear resistance to blessed objects or the name of Jesus, noting that the most convincing sign is "the presence of what appears as an independent, intelligent entity (or entities), and the expressed desire of this intelligence not to leave the afflicted."[15]

Dr. Siang-Yang Tan is the Senior Professor of Psychology in Fuller Seminary's Clinical Psychology Department. Tan, also a Fellow of the American Psychological Association (APA), writes the following:

> Some helpful criteria (though not foolproof) for discerning the presence of the demonic versus mental illness include the following: the afflicted person's strong, negative reaction to hearing the name "Jesus" (or the reading of Scripture or the singing of hymns); a foreboding or almost overwhelming sense of evil on the part of the therapist; the afflicted person's history of involvement with the occult and/or cults; and possibly an olfactory criterion involving a smell of sulfur or rotten eggs associated with the afflicted person.[16]

Pastors should not depend on Hollywood-style theatrics, but neither should we ignore the presence of consistent biblical patterns. When evaluated "with much prayer and dependence on the Holy Spirit and his gift of discerning of spirits," these signs can provide compelling evidence of severe demonization.[17]

The Guy Who Could Fly

Not long ago, I was talking with Dr. Joe Oden, director of the Assemblies of God World Prayer Center in Springfield, Missouri, about the difficulty of distinguishing between psychological symptoms and spiritual manifestations.

---

in at least 437, or 89 percent. Possession is a global phenomenon. Throughout her book, *Phenomenal Phenomena*, Dr. Vaughan explores findings from the field of global anthropology that demonstrate that the signs of demonic manifestations noted throughout the New Testament are well accounted for among people suffering from possession states throughout the world. The specific signs that she discusses are consistent with the signs noted in the *Rituale Romanum*.

15. Gallagher, "Case of Demonic Possession," 24.
16. Tan, *Counseling and Psychotherapy*, 405–6.
17. Tan, *Counseling and Psychotherapy*, 406.

At one point in the conversation, he asked me a pointed question: "Have you ever seen someone levitate during a demonic manifestation?"

I paused. It's not the kind of thing you say casually. But after a moment of reflection, I admitted, "Yes. Twice." Both events are burned into my memory, but one of them is especially vivid.

It was a normal weekday. I was at my desk when I received an urgent text from a man named Marvin. The message simply said: *"Help me."* Since Marvin was working in the sanctuary just down the hall, I remember thinking, "Why didn't he just come tell me what he needed?" Then, I walked into the sanctuary—and I understood.

Marvin was lying on the floor convulsing. The phone he'd just used to text me had been flung to the side. I didn't know what had triggered the episode, but I immediately recognized it as a demonic manifestation. As I knelt beside him, I placed my hand on his chest and rebuked the unclean spirit in Jesus's name. That's when it happened.

Marvin's entire body shot straight up into the air. I don't mean a subtle lift or an arched back—I mean he levitated. His whole body rose off the ground like a puppet on invisible strings. Instinctively, I reached out and caught him in mid-air. To this day, I believe that if I hadn't done so, he might have hit the ceiling.

In that moment, I had total clarity. This wasn't emotionalism, mental illness, or a nervous breakdown. This was demonic. I rebuked the spirit again, calling on the name of Jesus, and Marvin's body dropped to the floor. He wept, wailed, and trembled. As I knelt beside him and called his name, he slowly came to himself.

Later, Marvin shared more of his story. He'd suffered sexual abuse as a child. As he grew older, he struggled with confusion about his identity, battled intense depression, and at times flirted with thoughts of suicide. He had been fighting a spiritual war privately for years, all while sitting in church Sunday after Sunday.

I liked Marvin. He was sincere, kind, and faithful to church. Still, I had no idea the depth of what he was facing. He had never shared the extent of his pain—and I had never thought to ask.

Most people won't levitate to let you know they need help. In fact, spiritual warfare is seldom that clear cut. Dramatic moments like that one are rare, but they do happen. When they do, the need for spiritual intervention is immediate. If someone's body is being violently controlled or lifted off the ground during visible torment, you probably don't need to walk them through every step of the diagnostic process outlined in this book. At that point, it's wise to exercise the authority of Christ and address the spiritual attack head-on.

That said, not every case is so extreme. In most situations, demonic influence is more subtle. It hides beneath layers of trauma, shame, secrecy, and silence. That's why discernment matters. If we wait for someone to fly before we recognize their torment, we may miss the chance to help them earlier. Discernment must be relational and intentional. We must listen to stories, ask hard questions, and invite the Holy Spirit to reveal what's hidden.

Years later, long after his deliverance and healing journey began, Marvin and I were having lunch when he suddenly looked up and asked, "Did I really levitate that day—or was that just in my head? It felt like someone was picking me up off the ground." I looked him in the eyes and said, "No, Marvin. You actually flew."

Stories like Marvin's are unforgettable; they're also uncommon. For most people, the signs of demonic oppression or possession are less cinematic and more complex. That's why the next section will walk through the difficult, but necessary work of ruling out mental illness and trauma as primary causes before jumping to conclusions about demonization. Discerning the need for deliverance is not always obvious, but when we're committed to truth, compassion, and patience, we'll be far better equipped to help people find freedom.

Ruling Out Mental Illness and Trauma

As we discussed in chapter 5, wise pastors should rule out medical and psychological conditions that may mimic demonic behavior. These include:

- Bipolar Disorder
- Schizophrenia
- Dissociative Identity Disorder
- Thyroid Disease
- Diabetes
- Neurological Conditions[18]

18. Quay, *Minister's Manual*, 4; see also, Isaacs, *Revelations and Possession*, 119, 123; see also, Meier et al., *Blue Genes*, chap 8. Although it isn't discussed elsewhere in this

These conditions are real and often treatable. Dismissing them as merely demonic can lead to tragedy. However, equally dangerous is ignoring real spiritual torment under the label of mental illness. Some people suffer from both. That's why pastoral discernment must work hand-in-hand with mental health professionals.

Warning Against Rushed Diagnoses

Just because someone shakes, yells, or collapses does not mean they are possessed. These same reactions happen during panic attacks, trauma flashbacks, and intense grief. Don't rush. Don't label, and never, ever shame.

It's good to be passionate, but faith doesn't require volume. In the right context, it is appropriate to pray loudly, but shouting at traumatized people is seldom helpful. Even if your motive is right, it may do more harm than good. Instead, listen to them. Watch and pray, trusting the Spirit to reveal what is hidden.

The Goal Is Freedom, Not Just Diagnosis

At the end of the day, our calling is not to become spiritual diagnosticians—it's to become agents of Christ's healing and freedom. Diagnosis is a tool, not a trophy.

Much damage is done by careless suggestions that someone may be possessed. However, an equal amount of damage is likely done by careless suggestions of mental illness. Writing as a mental health professional about those in distress, Alexander DiChiara observes, "The pathologizing of a person's experience into such a disorder has detrimental effects on the person and alienates them further."[19] Neither pastors nor mental health professionals should hastily attach labels to people.

If someone is demonized, Jesus can set them free. If someone is traumatized, Jesus can heal their heart. If someone is mentally ill, Jesus can restore their hope and bring the right help into their life.

---

book, Exorcist and scholar, Mark Quay, lists untreated diabetes as a condition that can be misunderstood as demonic under the right circumstances.

19. DiChiara, "Dissociation, Possession, Or Otherwise," 5.

Our goal is not to get the label right. It's to get the person free. So, ask the right questions. Watch for the right signs. Walk in humility, and let the Holy Spirit be the one who makes the invisible clear.

When the Darkness Follows You Home

Tori, Tiffany, and Rebecca had been close friends for years. Drawn together by a shared fascination with horror movies and the supernatural, they often experimented with occult practices—dabbling in witchcraft, playing occult themed games, consuming books that glorified witchcraft, and most recently, obsessing over spirit animals or guides. One of them claimed to see a wolf-like creature that not only appeared to her but identified itself by name. All three occasionally attended church, but their spiritual explorations were far from innocent curiosity.

Everything began to change when Tori reached a breaking point. Convicted by the weight of her involvement in the occult and desperate for peace, she cried out to Jesus and had an experience in his presence that was like nothing she'd ever known. A spiritual battle erupted as demonic forces reacted to her desire to turn to Christ.

That same night, the three girls had planned a sleepover at Tiffany's house. While Tori was at church, Tiffany and Rebecca had watched the horror film *Child's Play*. But when Tori arrived, the spiritual atmosphere shifted dramatically. Rebecca claimed to see a spirit—what she believed was the ghost of a deceased relative—and in a moment of fear-tinged curiosity, she invited it in. Instantly, chaos erupted. Her body was thrown across the room. Scratches and bruises appeared spontaneously on her skin. Tiffany soon noticed the same marks on her own body. A dark figure was seen darting through the house. Disembodied voices and banging noises only intensified the fear. That's when they called me and my wife, pleading for help.

We prayed over the phone, rebuking the darkness. Tori, still fresh in her faith, joined us boldly—calling out to Jesus and rebuking the spirits. Tiffany followed, haltingly at first, then with growing faith. While the spiritual oppression relented to a degree, there was no lasting breakthrough.

The next day, they came to our home in desperation. As soon as we began to pray in person, all three girls collapsed—screaming, vomiting, and writhing on the floor. The scene was chaotic and deeply unsettling. Tiffany and Rebecca were gripped by violent convulsions, with new bruises appearing even as we watched. As we prayed, rebuking the demonic, we noticed a strange pattern: when one began to calm, another would erupt in emotional or physical distress. The battle seemed to pass between them like a storm looking for a weak place to land.

Finally, we stopped and led all three girls through a prayer of repentance and renunciation. We named their occult activities, denounced them before God, and declared Jesus's authority over their lives. As we prayed, peace settled over the room like a gentle wind after a storm.

What followed was revealing. One of the girls surrendered fully to Jesus and has continued walking with him to this day. Another remained active in the church for some time but later fell away—though years later, she reached out to say she had recommitted her life to Christ. The third, to my knowledge, never fully turned from the occult or gave her life to Jesus, at least not during that season.

Reflecting through the lens of Isaacs' diagnostic criteria, Rebecca clearly exhibited the markers of full-blown possession: a loss of bodily control, inability to think clearly or speak, trance-like states, voices, and hallucinations. Tiffany and Tori showed signs of serious oppression or obsession, though perhaps not possession in its most extreme form. I personally witnessed involuntary bodily reactions and trance states in both Rebecca and Tiffany. While psychological explanations may account for some responses, they do not explain everything—least of all the synchronized physical manifestations, the immediate reaction to prayer, or the lingering presence that several of us perceived in the room.

If I could revisit that moment today, I would approach some aspects differently—with greater spiritual precision and pastoral clarity. But even so, this encounter remains a sobering reminder: the spiritual world is not a playground, and there are real consequences to entertaining the demonic. Jesus is merciful, but the cost of flirting with darkness is high. Tori, Tiffany, and Rebecca's story stands as both a cautionary tale and a testimony—of deliverance, decision, and the unrelenting grace of God.

Their story is a vivid reminder of why discernment matters. Diagnosis is not about labeling—it's about guiding people toward lasting freedom. Tori's courage, Tiffany's openness, and Rebecca's resistance each teach us something different about the complexities of spiritual oppression and the importance of pastoral care. Using tools like Isaacs' criteria doesn't replace prayer or Spirit-led ministry—it enhances it. When we face cases like these, we must remember: the goal is not control, but freedom. Not fear, but faith. Not just casting out darkness—but calling people into the light of Christ, where true healing begins.

Questions to Discuss

1. Why is it helpful to use the term "demonized" rather than "possessed" in some ministry contexts, and how does this shift in language affect how we approach people in need of deliverance?
2. How can pastors and ministry leaders balance the need for spiritual discernment with the responsibility to rule out mental illness or trauma before diagnosing demonization?
3. In cases like Marvin's or Rebecca's, extreme manifestations made spiritual torment obvious. How should our approach differ when the signs are subtle or hidden?
4. What lessons can be drawn from the three "major doorways" to demonic influence—personal sin, trauma, and occult involvement—and how might ministry responses differ for each?
5. Tori, Tiffany, and Rebecca's story shows three different responses to deliverance ministry: surrender, partial openness, and resistance. What does this teach us about free will, spiritual warfare, and the limits of ministerial control?

Chapter 11

Unclean No More

The death, burial, and resurrection of Jesus Christ represent the decisive victory over the powers of darkness. The New Testament declares this triumph with clarity: "by canceling the record of debt that stood against us with its legal demands. This he set aside, nailing it to the cross. He disarmed the rulers and authorities and put them to open shame, by triumphing over them in him" (Col 2:14–15). The author of Hebrews echoes the same truth: "[H]e himself likewise partook of the same things, that through death he might destroy the one who has the power of death, that is, the devil, and deliver all those who through fear of death were subject to lifelong slavery" (Heb 2:14b–15). These scriptures remind us that New Testament deliverance ministry is not a fight *for* victory—it is an expression *of* victory. When individuals willingly submit to Jesus Christ through faith, the opportunities for healing, wholeness, and freedom are truly limitless.

Christ's Deliverance Ministry

Books like *The Deliverance Dialogues* can naturally raise a variety of questions in the minds of readers. Perhaps the most common question I get is this: If the things you are saying about deliverance are true, then why are the encounters in the New Testament short, verbal exchanges, after which demons are driven out through Christ's authority? Why don't we see this kind of evaluation of people's trauma and illnesses as part of the deliverance ministry of Christ and the apostles. My simple answer is—I believe that we do. The Gospels and the book of Acts describe the moment when demons are cast out as an expression of breathtaking power that is released from Heaven, leaving onlookers in awe of God's amazing grace, love, and presence. This remains the common experience of those who are involved in deliverance and exorcism ministry today.

The New Testament doesn't provide every detail about the conversations that surrounded its exorcism narratives. We don't know how long those exchanges took, and we don't know what all was said. What we do know is that the early church was deeply committed to discipleship, so I am confident that there were ongoing conversations about how to live in freedom. In fact, the New Testament is filled with guidance on how to endure spiritual warfare while resisting demonic attacks. Before examining some contemporary models of deliverance, let's take a moment and evaluate some of the dialogue that surrounds the biblical encounters.

From Deliverance to Discipleship

I have often heard people claim that demons always fled as soon as Jesus spoke. Mark's account of Christ's showdown with Legion directly reveals otherwise.

> And when he saw Jesus from afar, he ran and fell down before him. And crying out with a loud voice, he said, "What have you to do with me, Jesus, Son of the Most High God? I adjure you by God, do not torment me." For he was saying to him, "Come out of the man, you unclean spirit!" (Mark 5:6–7)

The demons spoke through the man, begging Jesus not to torment them, while He "was saying . . . come out of the man." While Jesus was speaking, the demons were protesting. It didn't end there. The entire exchange where Jesus asks for the unclean spirit's name and they request to go into the pigs all happened after He had told the spirit to come out (vv. 9–13). Does Jesus have absolute authority? Yes! Nonetheless, the spirits did not leave as soon as He spoke.

When the community arrives to witness the man's transformation, they find him "sitting there, clothed, and in his right mind" (Mark 5:15). Sitting at the rabbi's feet was the posture of a student in the ancient world. Jesus was with him long enough for the man to get dressed, sit down at his feet, and learn. He began discipling him as soon as the demons left. The conversation continued as Jesus spoke with him about his future, encouraging him to go home and tell his friends what God had done for him (vv. 18–19).

A Conversation with Dad

Mark's account of a boy who is mute, deaf, and suffers from seizures is especially striking. The conversation between Jesus and the boy's father begins because the disciples couldn't liberate the child (Mark 9:18). Jesus starts by interviewing the boy's father about his condition (vv. 17–18). This is the same approach that many deliverance ministers take today, especially within a pastoral counseling setting. When the child is brought before Jesus, demonic manifestations begin suddenly, but to the reader's surprise, Jesus does not immediately cast out the spirit. Instead, he returns to his conversation with the boy's dad (vs. 21). While the boy convulses and foams at the mouth, Jesus asks questions about how long the spirit has been there, how it has affected him, and whether the dad has faith (vv. 20–24). Although we don't know how long this exchange lasted, we do know that it took long enough for a crowd to gather (vs. 25). Jesus commands the spirit to come out, and although it does, the text clearly documents its resistance. The unclean spirit comes out, but only "after crying out and convulsing him terribly" (vs. 26). When the spectacle is finally over, the boy lays on the ground like a dead man, and the text indicates that Jesus heals him while lifting him up (vv. 26–27). This was a powerful deliverance, but it was hardly instantaneous.

Prayerless and Faithless Disciples

The disciples were no strangers to deliverance ministry. They witnessed Jesus confront unclean spirits time and again—and they themselves were entrusted with that same authority. Matthew 10:1 recalls the moment Jesus summoned them and "gave them authority over unclean spirits." They weren't inexperienced. They weren't uninformed. Yet in this particular case, they found themselves powerless in the face of a demonized child—and the child's father was left disillusioned and desperate (Mark 9:18, 24).

After Jesus intervened and dramatically set the boy free, the disciples came to him privately and asked what surely felt like a reasonable question:

"Why couldn't we drive it out?" (Mark 9:28). Jesus didn't soften his response. "Because of your unbelief," He said plainly (Matt 17:20, MEV). That had to sting. Perhaps the disciples expected Jesus to say this demon required a higher level of authority or a special spiritual rank. Instead, He went straight to the root of the issue: their lack of faith.

But Jesus didn't stop at diagnosis—He gave them the prescription. "This kind does not go out except by prayer and fasting" (Matt 17:21; cf. Mark 9:29, MEV).[1] That statement reveals something crucial about spiritual authority: it must be cultivated. The disciples had been given authority, but their unbelief kept them from operating in it. The power they once walked in had been compromised—not because the power source had changed, but because their connection to it had weakened.

The same danger faces us today. If we choose comfort over consecration—prayerlessness over intimacy with God—then we too will lack the power to confront darkness when it matters most. Spiritual authority is not a once-for-all impartation that requires no upkeep. It must be stewarded through communion with the Father, consistency in the Word, and a life marked by prayer and fasting.

When we become prayerless, we also become powerless. And when believers are powerless, the oppressed remain bound. Deliverance doesn't come through good intentions, clever words, or ministerial titles. It comes through people who have been with Jesus, who live in his presence, and who walk in his authority. That kind of authority is not just delegated—it is cultivated.

Christ's Methodology

The New Testament describes Jesus casting demons out of large numbers of people. In most of those accounts, we know virtually nothing about the details. What is notable is that the Gospels supply seven full exorcism narratives, some which describe lengthy interactions like those shared above. Christ has absolute authority over evil spirits. They are terrified of him, but some of them still pushed back when He commanded them to leave. Based on these narratives, we have every reason to expect that Jesus regularly asked questions, evaluated situations, and designed his interventions accordingly.

Today's pastors should learn from Christ's methodology. He didn't begin by screaming at demons. He interacted with the afflicted humans

1. The ESV does not include the reference to fasting, but simply says, "This kind cannot be driven out by anything but prayer" (Mark 9:29).

and their families, and when the encounters ended, he took time to care for them and teach them. I often tell ministers that if we walk in Christ's authority and invest sufficient time in prayer and fasting, then we can be confident as we cast out demons. Within that confidence, there should be no reason to continually repeat ourselves after commanding a spirit to come out in Jesus's Name. When possible, we should ask the questions that are necessary to get a full picture of the individual's struggle. When we command the spirit to leave, we should expect it to depart within several minutes, and if it doesn't, then I recommend asking the Holy Spirit for further insights rather than just leaving someone suffering through violent manifestations.

When it comes to helping people experience this freedom from demonic influence, no single model fits every individual or every pastoral situation. The landscape of deliverance ministry is as diverse as the people seeking help. Some models emphasize dramatic manifestations and power encounters. Others focus on inner healing, identity restoration, and integration. Each model carries strengths and potential weaknesses. In the remainder of this chapter, we'll evaluate some of the most prominent models, draw out best practices, and offer practical recommendations for pastors desiring to minister wisely and effectively.

The Healing Power of Community

Deliverance is about more than the absence of torment; it is about the restoration of wholeness—peace with God, peace with self, and peace with others. Throughout the Synoptic Gospels, those delivered by Jesus are not merely freed from unclean spirits; they are reintegrated into life-giving relationships and meaningful community.

The man tormented in the synagogue (Mark 1:21–28; Luke 4:31–37) is no longer a disruption to public worship—he is now a participant, seated among others in peace. The mute demoniac (Matt 9:32–34) and the blind and mute man (Matt 12:22–29) receive the gift of speech and sight—restoring their ability to connect and communicate with others. The Syrophoenician woman (Matt 15:21–28) returns home to a calm and sane daughter, and the father of the epileptic boy (Mark 9:14–29) takes home a son who is no longer a danger to himself. The woman afflicted for eighteen years (Luke 13:10–17) is embraced by the presence of Christ in the synagogue, not as a spectacle, but as a daughter of Abraham. And perhaps most memorably, the man from the tombs—the one who called himself "Legion"—is commissioned by Jesus to return home and testify among his friends (Mark 5:19). Isolation gives way to reintegration. These are not just stories of liberation; they are stories of restoration.

Jesus did not liberate people only to send them off in solitude. Like the cleansed lepers of Levitical law, those who were set free from unclean spirits were meant to be restored to the covenant community. The social restoration that follows deliverance becomes the next phase of healing. Community becomes the soil in which lasting transformation takes root.

Modern deliverance testimonies often echo this same truth. In her research on individuals who experienced significant deliverance, Alyson Barry notes that these individuals didn't remain silent about what they had endured—they shared it. She writes, "Feeling as if they are a part of a supportive group of people may facilitate healing for these individuals. This shared understanding seems to have led to the development of what I might call a deliverance culture."[2] Within these groups, there is a common language, shared beliefs, and mutual support.[3] These communities provide something that many of the formerly demonized had never experienced before: belonging.

For people who have lived fractured by trauma, alienated by affliction, or misunderstood by both secular and religious institutions, finding a community that understands their journey is deeply healing. Psychiatrist M. Scott Peck once wrote, "It [community] also has an almost mystical healing power that often plays a more important role in a successful exorcism than does the exorcist him- or herself."[4] While the act of casting out an unclean spirit is critical, what follows is equally important. Healing requires a safe place to process, to be known, and to grow.

The church of Jesus Christ should be that place.

When the church becomes a community of healing—offering belonging to the broken, safety to the tormented, and dignity to the demonized—it lives into its highest calling. In a world that increasingly marginalizes the spiritually afflicted, the church can be a sanctuary for both liberation and integration. The healing power of community is not optional—it is essential. Without it, many will experience freedom only to fall again into isolation. But with it, they may not only be set free. . . they may finally become whole.

2. Barry, "Qualitative Analysis," 129–30.

3. Barry, "Qualitative Analysis," 129–30.

4. Peck, *Glimpses of the Devil*, 191.

Contemporary Deliverance Models

Bull's Therapeutic Exorcism Model for the Possession Form Dissociative Identity Disorder

While some exorcists have warned against taking people with dissociative disorders through deliverance, Psychologist Dr. Dennis Bull asserts that it is possible to do so safely.[5] Bull writes,

> Exorcisms appear to cause problems for two main reasons. First, exorcisms tend to be done by religious people with little or no understanding of dissociative disorders and/or psychological dynamics. It is damaging when psychological constructs such as alter personalities are assumed to be demons by those doing exorcism. Second, when done by some in Christian ministry, exorcisms tend to be practiced in controlling and demeaning ways; they tend to be done "to" the patient with little or no cooperation on the part of the patient. This is often experienced as revictimization by the patient.[6]

Bull's model is particularly designed with clinical sensitivity. It should be considered in situations where individuals have been diagnosed with DID but are also experiencing paranormal activity that cannot be attributed to a psychological condition. After emphasizing the need to be gentle and non-coercive, Bull lists three steps to therapeutic exorcism:[7]

1. "**Collaborate** with the patient. . . ."[8] Deliverance ministers and therapists should work with patients to determine what needs to be cast out. This is a good time to discuss what the patient feels, hears, and sees. There may be images that do not appear demonic to the patient but do appear that way to others. When dealing with DID, it is vital to trust the patient's sense about things.

5. MacNutt, *Deliverance from Evil Spirits*, 83; see also, Friesen, *Uncovering the Mystery of MPD*, 246. MacNutt strongly cautions against using exorcistic techniques with people who may have DID, warning of potentially catastrophic consequences. His statements are based on research presented by Dr. James Friesen, cited here as well. Dennis Bull, referencing the same published work by Friesen, offers balance to the conversation by explaining why exorcism can cause damage and how to avoid doing so.

6. Bull, "Phenomenological Model," 132.

7. Bull, "Phenomenological Model," 134.

8. Bull, "Phenomenological Model," 135. The bold font is mine.

2. **Ask** the patient if he/she believes in a power that is stronger than their demon.[9] Those with DID typically believe that their tormenter is supernatural. Therefore, it must also be confronted supernaturally. For ministers, this is an excellent time to encourage the individual to call on the name of Christ. Bull writes, "It seems ironic that calling on a higher power is standard fare for work with patients who have addictions, yet it is frowned upon and somehow seen as illegitimate for other kinds of psychiatric disorders."[10] This is a vital insight.
3. **Encourage** "the patient to take control of expelling the demon."[11] While the one leading this deliverance session may offer help when needed, the primary goal is to offer encouragement and guidance to the patient. Bull learned from "experience that when an alter is banned, patients report that it feels like a part of themselves is missing, but when an entity is banned, they feel relief. The ultimate decision must be the patient's."[12]

Dr. Bull's model of therapeutic exorcism offers a way forward for ministers and therapists who want to help but also recognize the risk of harm. By recognizing DID as a mental illness that may alternatively be viewed as a possession state, Bull's model paves the way for a healthy blend of liberation from demons and integration of the human psyche. The model avoids coercion and highlights agency, offering a framework that is pastorally sensitive and therapeutically responsible. It recognizes that healing is not just about casting out, but also about integrating the fragmented self.

Recommendation: Bull's approach is best suited for collaborative settings where deliverance ministers and mental health professionals are working together. It serves as an ideal bridge between spiritual authority and clinical caution.

9. Bull, "Phenomenological Model," 135.
10. Bull, "Phenomenological Model," 134.
11. Bull, "Phenomenological Model," 134.
12. Bull, "Phenomenological Model," 135. As a reminder, "alter" refers to multiple expressions of the individual's own consciousness. Someone who endured severe childhood abuse may have one personality that is quiet and timid and another that is loud and aggressive. These are not demons, but alternate expressions of the individual's mind that fragmented into numerous pieces as an act of self-protection. Such things must be healed rather than exorcised. At the same time, an "entity" is likely perceived by the sufferer as a demon or monster and needs to be confronted. Although this is a deliverance model, it is uniquely designed for DID sufferers and is distinct from how deliverance would typically be carried out.

Bottari's Ten Step Model

At the height of the revival in Argentina, Pablo Bottari emerged as a trusted and compassionate voice in the ministry of deliverance. Working closely with Evangelist Carlos Annacondia, Bottari became a shepherd of the broken, ministering not only with power, but with deep tenderness. By the time his book *Free in Christ* was published, Bottari claimed that more than one million individuals had passed through Annacondia's massive deliverance tent, thirty thousand of whom Bottari prayed with personally.[13]

He described scenes that seemed lifted from another world—moments of spiritual warfare breaking into the physical realm. In his words:

> In the crusade services, Evangelist Carlos Annacondia rebuked demons, and individuals who appeared completely insane began to shriek, howl and collapse to the ground, exhibiting spectacular manifestations. They were taken away by groups of stretcher-bearers and ushers who carried them out in convulsions, spasms, crying, vomiting and, in some cases, violent fits. It looked like a scene from Dante—an invisible battlefield. . . . In the deliverance tent, I watched those who entered screaming and disfigured leave with a radiant glow of peaceful calm.[14]

While many deliverance models exist, Bottari's stands apart for its clarity, structure, and compassion. His method reflects the belief that even amid demonic chaos, God desires to bring peace, order, and restoration. His ten-step model has now been taught across the globe, helping multitudes experience true freedom in Christ.

The Ten Steps of Deliverance

Bottari's model is divided into two phases. The first four steps are specific to moments when a demonic spirit is actively manifesting. The remaining six are applicable to the broader process of leading someone into sustained healing and liberation.

1. **Make Sure the Person Is Manifesting**

   Demonization should never be assumed. Before proceeding with deliverance, the minister should discern whether a spirit is indeed

13. Bottari, *Free in Christ*, 19.
14. Bottari, *Free in Christ*, 5–7.

present and manifesting. Not every case of distress is the result of demonization. Wisdom must guide each step.

2. **Take Authority in the Name of Jesus and Bind the Spirit**

   Bottari emphasizes the power of Christ's Name as the authority that binds unclean spirits.[15] The moment a demon begins to manifest, it must be bound—stopping its influence and disruption.

3. **Bring the Person Back to Consciousness**

   Often, during a manifestation, the individual may appear disoriented or dissociated. The minister should gently call the person back to awareness, affirming their dignity and role in the process.

4. **Ask If They Want to Be Free**

   Deliverance is never forced. The person must desire freedom and express their consent. Bottari is clear that deliverance is most effective when the person participates by faith and choice.

5. **Present the Plan of Salvation**

   Deliverance is not just about expelling demons; it is about reconciling the individual to God. If the person has not yet trusted Christ, this is the moment to share the gospel and invite them into relationship with Jesus.

6. **Discover the Areas of Bondage as Consequences of Sin**

   Freedom requires understanding the root causes of oppression. These may include personal sin, trauma, unforgiveness, or generational patterns. Bottari's approach here is pastoral and respectful, helping the person recognize areas that need healing or repentance.

7. **Lead the Person to Renounce the Ties That Cause Oppression**

   Verbal renunciation of ungodly ties is a powerful spiritual act. Bottari leads people in specific prayers that reject past agreements, occult involvement, and hidden sins that may have opened the door to demonic influence.

15. Although many scholars challenge this usage of the word "bind," it is how Bottari and many throughout the Pentecostal and Charismatic movement use the word. Whether one agrees with the language of "binding" demons through prayer, the general principal of exercising a restraining authority over demons through Christ's power is well established in the Gospels and Acts.

8. **Take Authority in the Name of Jesus, Casting Out the Spirit**

   Once the groundwork of confession and renunciation has been laid, the spirit is commanded to leave in Jesus's Name. This does not have to be a chaotic spectacle; Bottari's ministry is marked by calm authority and reliance on the Holy Spirit.

9. **Give Thanks to God for Deliverance**

   Thanksgiving is an essential part of deliverance. It acknowledges that freedom is not achieved by human effort, but by the power and grace of God through Jesus Christ.

10. **Lead the Person to Pray for the Fullness of the Holy Spirit**

    Deliverance creates space—space that must be filled. Bottari concludes by leading individuals to pray for the infilling of the Holy Spirit, inviting God's presence to dwell within and empower them to walk in newness of life.[16]

Pablo Bottari's model is rooted in scripture, humility, and grace. It offers both structure and sensitivity, reflecting a belief that deliverance is not merely about expelling evil but about restoring wholeness. His gentle approach has brought peace to thousands, and his model continues to serve as a trusted guide for ministers of inner healing and spiritual warfare around the world.

Recommendation: Bottari's method can be used in both individual and group ministry settings, especially when dealing with those who are actively manifesting. However, ministers should be trained to avoid sensationalism and to pursue peace-filled, Spirit-led intervention.

Lozano's Unbound Model—Five Keys

Neil Lozano, deeply influenced by Bottari, developed a model of deliverance around five simple but profound steps:

1. Repentance and faith
2. Forgiveness

16. Bottari, *Free in Christ*, 87, 97, 102, 106, 110, 113, 140, 147, 152. The ten steps are adapted from the pages cited. Although I have mostly kept his language, I have added some slight adaptations for clarity. Also, in step 8, Bottari simply repeats "Take Authority in the Name of Jesus," which is almost identical to his step 2. I have added "Casting Out the Spirit" to step 8, as that is Bottari's explanation and application of step 8.

3. Renunciation
4. Standing in Christ's authority
5. Receiving the Father's blessing[17]

Lozano's Unbound model is particularly helpful for those who have suffered emotional wounds, harbor unforgiveness, or feel spiritually bound without overt demonic manifestations. He prioritizes love and dignity, values that he largely credits Bottari with teaching him. He writes that Bottari, "taught me how to pray for people so that, if they did not get free right away, they would still feel loved. He taught me how to minimize the physical manifestations of evil that people are often subjected to in deliverance."[18] This is not an approach for showy deliverance. It is a pastoral, healing model that offers deep discipleship and long-term freedom.

Recommendation: Unbound is ideal for church-based counseling, small group ministry, and pre-deliverance preparation. It avoids triggering trauma and allows time for God to do deeper healing.

A Father's Blessing: Barbara's Breakthrough

Barbara didn't grow up in a Christian home. Her earliest memories were clouded with screaming voices and cigarette smoke so thick she could barely see through it. Loneliness was her constant companion, and her transient childhood made it difficult to form lasting friendships. When she finally began attending church as a child, it was the first place she truly felt loved. By her teenage years, the weight of rejection and emotional isolation pressed in hard.

Like many young women desperate for affection, Barbara found herself in a relationship with a boy who offered the illusion of love but carried darkness within him. He drank heavily and practiced a form of sorcery that was openly malicious. His "magic" was used to curse and control, and when Barbara became sexually involved with him, the consequences were devastating. Though she hadn't wanted to cross that line, her longing for affirmation led her to believe that physical intimacy might secure his love. It didn't. Instead, he slandered her publicly, ruining her reputation and compounding her pain.

17. Lozano, *Unbound*, 57.
18. Lozano, *Unbound*, 177.

Years later, after falling in love and marrying her best friend, the real unraveling began. Oddly enough, it was after she finally felt safe that the inner torment intensified. Panic attacks, depression, terrifying visions, and dissociative episodes began disrupting her life and her marriage. Though she pursued counseling and tried various medications, nothing brought lasting relief. She prayed, read her Bible, and served faithfully at church—but something still wasn't right.

Barbara began attending the church I pastored in her early thirties. Though she smiled and served with joy, the spiritual heaviness surrounding her was unmistakable. I prayed for her on one occasion, and she was suddenly thrown to the ground, her body contorting and her voice screaming uncontrollably. I rebuked what I believed to be demonic spirits and prayed fervently. There was momentary peace, but no lasting breakthrough.

That changed when Evangelist Tom McNaughton and his wife, Pat, came to hold revival services at our church. The McNaughtons had a robust deliverance ministry and saw God work miracles that stagger the imagination. Under their leadership, our congregation experienced revival services that lasted for three weeks and then continued for another six at what is now Link Church in Clarksville, AR. Somewhere in the middle of that move of God, I introduced Barbara to the McNaughtons, hoping they might have wisdom I lacked.

They agreed to meet with her in private. As they prayed, they encountered the same level of intense physical and emotional manifestation that I had seen before. The prayer session went on for hours until everyone was exhausted. Then came the turning point.

Tom paused, looked directly into Barbara's eyes, and gently said, "I feel like God told me to hug you the way your father would have hugged you." Barbara welcomed this gentle, loving gesture.

It was a simple act, but one profoundly guided by the Holy Spirit. What Tom didn't know was that Barbara's father had passed away—and to her knowledge, had never once hugged her. As Tom embraced her and Pat prayed softly beside them, Barbara experienced something that defied natural explanation. She broke into tears, and through her sobs she recognized a familiar smell—her father. He had been gone for years, but in that moment, it was as though he was the one hugging her. Whether this was a supernatural encounter or a Spirit-empowered perception, the impact on Barbara was undeniable.

It was a holy moment.

As Tom spoke a father's blessing over her life—telling her she was loved, accepted, and cherished—Barbara was finally able to receive what her soul had long craved. A wave of supernatural peace swept over her. The torment lifted. The pain lost its grip. For the first time in years, she was free.

That blessing changed everything. Barbara was instantly healed of a chronic medical condition. Her relationship with her husband blossomed. The terror that had stalked her was gone, replaced by the joy of someone who had encountered not just deliverance, but love. Real love. Healing love. A Father's love.

What years of counseling, medication, and even attempted exorcism could not accomplish, one Spirit-empowered embrace released: a revelation of the Father's heart.

It should be noted that a hug of this sort could be perceived in various ways, depending on the cultural context. Physical touch should generally be limited in pastoral counseling settings. Although God used this hug as a conduit of healing for Barbara, wisdom and discretion are vital.

Lozano's *Unbound* model highlights the power of the Father's blessing for a reason. Deliverance is not just about rejecting darkness; it is about receiving identity. It is about belonging. Barbara didn't just cast out lies. She received the truth, and in doing so, she was restored.

SOZO's Four Doors Model

Another prominent global deliverance ministry that emerged in recent decades is SOZO, a name derived from the Greek word for salvation and deliverance. The SOZO ministry began in 1987 as a direct outgrowth of Pablo Bottari's Ten Steps to Freedom. In their book *Sozo: Saved—Healed—Delivered: A Journey into Freedom with the Father, Son, and Holy Spirit*, founders Dawna De Silva and Teresa Liebscher reflect on their early days in ministry:

> When the Sozo Ministry began in 1987, the only tool we knew to use was Pablo Bottari's Ten Steps to Freedom. Since then, we have moved away from using the Ten Steps and have instead developed the Four Doors.[19]

Although the ministry eventually moved away from Bottari's formal methodology, it retained the essence of his insights. Most notably, Bottari identified four primary "entrances" through which the demonic realm

19. Liebscher and De Silva, *SOZO*, 109.

gains access to individuals: fear, hatred or bitterness, sexual sin, and occult activity. The Four Doors framework is built around these categories and serves as a diagnostic and prayer tool to uncover areas of spiritual bondage.

The Four Doors

The Four Doors model is a simple but profound metaphor. Each "door" represents a spiritual gateway—an area of personal vulnerability where demonic influence may gain entry. Understanding these doors helps individuals close off access to the enemy and reclaim territory for the Lord.

1. **Fear**

   This door includes worry, unbelief, a need for control, anxiety, isolation, apathy, and various addictions such as drug and alcohol abuse. These manifestations often stem from unresolved trauma or a worldview rooted in insecurity rather than trust in God.[20]

2. **Hatred / Bitterness**

   When the heart is embittered, it becomes fertile ground for demonic oppression. Inside this door lie envy, gossip, slander, rage, and even self-hatred or feelings of worthlessness. These are corrosive attitudes that not only wound others but damage the soul from within.[21]

3. **Sexual Sin**

   This door includes both consensual and non-consensual sexual activity outside of God's design. Adultery, pornography, fornication, sexual fantasy, molestation, rape, and other forms of sexual brokenness can open one's life to torment and shame—along with deeper spiritual bondage.[22]

4. **Occult**

   Engagement with supernatural forces outside of God's authority is perhaps the most obvious doorway to demonic influence. This

20. Liebscher and De Silva, *SOZO*, 109.

21. Liebscher and De Silva, *SOZO*, 112.

22. Liebscher and De Silva, *SOZO*, 116. A word of explanation concerning SOZO's definition of sexual sin is in order. As the authors mention non-consensual sex as a form of sexual sin, I wish to clarify that these are sins committed by the perpetrator against the victim. They do not represent sins on the part of the victim. As traumatizing experiences for the victim, they often represent areas where inner healing is needed, but victims do not need to repent for things done to them.

includes astrology, fortune-telling, tarot cards, séances, Ouija boards, coven participation, spell casting, and all forms of witchcraft. Even more subtle forms of manipulation can function as entry points.[23]

By identifying which doors have been opened—whether knowingly or unknowingly—SOZO ministers guide individuals through a process of repentance, forgiveness, and inner healing. The result is not merely the eviction of demonic influence, but the transformation of the heart through connection with the Father, Son, and Holy Spirit.

A Journey into Wholeness

What sets the SOZO ministry apart is its integrative and relational approach. The goal is not simply deliverance, but restoration of relationship with God and healing of the inner person. In contrast to models that focus exclusively on casting out demons, SOZO emphasizes emotional healing, confession, listening prayer, and receiving truth from God to replace lies rooted in past trauma or sin.

Though it no longer uses Bottari's formal Ten Steps, the Four Doors model is a clear continuation of his foundational insights, adapted for modern ministry contexts. It has been implemented in churches and ministries around the world and continues to bring freedom to those seeking wholeness in Christ.

Recommendation: Sozo's diagnostic tool can enhance any deliverance model by providing a practical structure for identifying root issues. However, it should always be paired with sound biblical teaching and pastoral oversight.

Tan's Seven Step Inner Healing Process

Though not strictly a deliverance model, Dr. Tan's seven-step inner healing process demonstrates the power of integrative healing alongside deliverance ministry. Tan describes "inner-healing prayer" as "a distinctively Christian type of prayer that can also be used as a spiritual intervention. . . ."[24] Although Tan notes that "at times a Christian therapist may need to deal with

23. Liebscher and De Silva, *SOZO,* 120.

24. Tan, *Counseling and Psychotherapy*, 419.

an obviously demonized client by praying a prayer of deliverance," there are times when integrative healing offers a more impactful approach.[25]

Tan describes his seven-step inner healing model in this way:

1. **Begin with prayer for protection from evil**; ask for the power and healing ministry of the Holy Spirit to take control of the session.
2. **Guide the client into a relaxed state**, usually by brief relaxation strategies (e.g., slow and deep breathing, calming self-talk, pleasant imagery, prayer, and Bible imagery).
3. **Guide the client to focus attention on a painful past event** or traumatic experience, to feel deeply the pain, hurt, anger, and so forth.
4. **Prayerfully ask the Lord, by the power of the Holy Spirit, to come to the client and minister his comfort, love, and healing grace** (even gentle rebuke where necessary). It may be imagery of Jesus or other healing imagery, music (song/hymn), Scriptures, a sense of the Spirit's presence or warmth, or other manifestation of the Spirit's working. No specific guided imagery or visualization is provided or directively given at this point.
5. **Wait quietly upon the Lord** to minister to the client with his healing grace and truth. Guide and speak only if necessary and led by the Holy Spirit. In order to follow or track with the client, the counselor will periodically and gently ask, "What's happening? What are you feeling or experiencing now?"
6. **Close in prayer**.
7. **Debrief and discuss** the inner-healing prayer experience with the client.[26]

Recommendation: Dr. Siang-Yang Tan's seven-step inner-healing prayer process is less directive than other models like SOZO, making it highly adaptable in pastoral counseling and prayer ministry. It emphasizes waiting on the Holy Spirit to minister directly to the counselee, avoiding coercion or over-imagination. At the same time, it requires pastoral discernment, spiritual maturity, and special care when walking with trauma survivors.

25. Tan, *Counseling and Psychotherapy*, 424.

26. Tan, *Counseling and Psychotherapy*, 419–20. The bold font is mine.

Toward a Harmonized Model—Liberation + Integration

The most effective deliverance ministries are those that liberate the soul and integrate the self. While some traditions emphasize casting demons out, and others focus on healing wounds within, these two approaches need not compete. In truth, they are complementary—and often inseparable.

Allyson Barry's qualitative analysis affirms that successful deliverance ministry frequently includes:

- Restoring personal agency through spiritual intervention[27]
- Facilitating self-integration, especially in cases involving trauma[28]
- Creating safe communities where individuals can tell their stories without fear or shame[29]

As the literature and lived experience both reveal, the most fruitful ministries are those that confront the demonic, disciple the individual, and reintegrate them into the Body of Christ. No single deliverance model offers a universal template, yet each one reflects glimpses of what becomes possible when we minister with reverence, structure, and Spirit-led compassion.

The challenge facing today's church is not to pick sides between methods, but to embrace principles that mirror the heart of Christ—truth, grace, authority, and love. In the next chapter, we'll explore how these principles converge in a new framework: the **Intensive Sanctification Model**—designed not merely to cast out, but to build up.

Questions to Discuss

1. How has media, particularly films like *The Exorcist*, shaped public expectations about demonization, and in what ways can those expectations hinder effective ministry?
2. The criteria laid out by Isaacs, Gallagher, and Tan offer measurable indicators of possession. How can these tools help us avoid both false positives and false negatives in diagnosis?

27. Barry, "Qualitative Analysis," 108, 128.
28. Barry, "Qualitative Analysis," 95.
29. Barry, "Qualitative Analysis," 129–30.

3. The chapter outlines three primary doorways to demonization—personal sin, trauma, and occult involvement. How might ministry approaches differ for each doorway?
4. In Marvin's and the Tori/Tiffany/Rebecca stories, the manifestations ranged from subtle oppression to extreme possession. How can we train ourselves to discern cases that require immediate intervention from those needing long-term pastoral care?
5. The chapter warns that diagnosis is a tool, not a trophy. What does this mean for how we talk to those we suspect are demonized, and how do we keep the focus on freedom rather than labels?

Chapter 12

The Journey to Freedom

When individuals seek relief from spiritual torment, true deliverance is not merely about expelling darkness—it is about guiding them into the light of Christ. This chapter presents a process that I have developed to help people experience lasting freedom. This approach integrates both liberating and restorative elements, drawing from the ministry of Jesus and the apostles, while incorporating the strengths of the models discussed in chapter 11.

Steps of Freedom

The following steps offer a biblical, pastoral, and Spirit-led pathway toward wholeness and spiritual breakthrough.

Step One: Begin with the Lordship of Jesus

Before anything else, declare and celebrate the unmatched authority of Jesus Christ. The battle is already won because "in him dwells all the fullness of the Godhead bodily" and "He disarmed principalities and powers, making a public spectacle of them" (Col 2:9, 15). Deliverance doesn't begin with a demon—it begins with Jesus.

Step Two: Speak of God's Love and His Desire to Deliver

People often come to deliverance feeling condemned. Remind them of God's deep love: "While we were yet sinners, Christ died for us" (Rom 5:8). The goal is not punishment, but restoration. The Father desires wholeness more than we desire relief.

Step Three: Lead Them Through Intensive Sanctification

Freedom isn't always instant. Use the Intensive Sanctification Model (ISM) to address roots, wounds, patterns, and strongholds. This model provides a framework for deep, Spirit-led healing and inner transformation.

Step Four: Command Unclean Spirits to Leave

If demonic presence is identified, and repentance and renunciation have taken place, command the spirits to leave in Jesus's name (Mark 16:17). There is no need to shout or show bravado. The authority is in his name.

Step Five: Invite the Holy Spirit to Fill the Empty Places

Once the stronghold has been broken, the heart must be filled. Invite the Holy Spirit to take residence, and pray for the fruit of the Spirit to be formed in the person's life (Matt 12:43–45).

Step Six: Walk With Them Beyond the Moment

Deliverance is a doorway, not the finish line. Provide follow-up, ongoing pastoral care, and solid biblical teaching. Help them get connected to a life-giving church community (Mark 5:15).

The Intensive Sanctification Model (ISM)

When I was a kid, commercials were just part of watching TV. There was no Netflix, no DVR, no ad-free streaming—just the show you wanted to watch and the commercials you had to sit through. One of my favorites advertised a stain remover called *Shout*. Each ad followed a familiar pattern:

a voice shouted the name of something that caused a stain—grass! mud! ketchup!—and just when it seemed like the stain would never come out, *Shout* detergent was applied and—voilà—it disappeared. The catchphrase stuck in my mind: "Can't get it out? Shout it out!"[1]

In my early days of pastoral ministry, I confess that I spent a lot more time shouting at demons than I did listening to the people I was trying to help. My heart was full of zeal, but my wisdom was still catching up. Over time, as our team saw more and more people experience genuine freedom, I noticed a consistent pattern. Breakthroughs happened when we:

1. Took time to truly understand their story
2. Received a plan from the Holy Spirit
3. Led them through a deep time of repentance and renunciation
4. Declared the Name of Jesus with love, grace, and confidence

When these four things happened, there was often no need to shout. Jesus did the heavy lifting.

As I continued in ministry, I developed spiritual rhythms that consistently bore fruit—but I realized they weren't easy to teach or reproduce. And while my wife and I are deeply committed to helping people, we can only minister to so many ourselves. That's when the Lord reminded me of Ephesians 4: our calling is not just to minister but to *equip others* to minister.

So, I began reflecting on the process. What made it work? It wasn't just the use of spiritual gifts—though words of knowledge, wisdom, and discernment were often present. It was dialogue. Dialogue with the Holy Spirit. Dialogue with the person seeking freedom. Dialogue with our ministry team. In these Spirit-led conversations, God spoke, lies were broken, hearts were opened, and miracles happened.

But for many people, this kind of conversation doesn't come naturally. They're unsure what to ask, what to say, or how to pray. That's why I developed the **Intensive Sanctification Model (ISM)**—a dialogue-based approach to helping people encounter Jesus Christ in ways that bring freedom, healing, and wholeness.

Why the name? Let's break it down:

1. Shout Laundry Stain Remover Commercial, "Shout It Out," 1992.

- **Intensive**: These are not casual conversations. The questions you'll ask go deep. They are personal, probing, and sometimes painful. But they are also life-giving.
- **Sanctification**: This process leads people to separate from what defiles and draw closer to what makes them whole. It is about cleansing, devotion, and transformation.
- **Model**: It's designed to be teachable, adaptable, and reproducible—so that others can learn to walk people through it, too.

I chose not to call it a "Deliverance Model," because not everyone who seeks help is demonized in the classical sense. But everyone needs sanctification. Everyone needs to confront truth, apply the blood of Jesus, and invite the Holy Spirit to fill the spaces once dominated by pain, lies, or shame. In the New Testament, sanctification comes by the *truth*, the *blood*, and the *Spirit*—and it is received by *faith*.

This takes the pressure off us as ministers. We are not saviors—we are facilitators of sacred encounters. Deliverance doesn't come through shouting; it comes through Jesus. And the Intensive Sanctification Model is one way we can lead people to him.

You will notice that in the "Steps of Freedom" outlined above, "Lead them through the Intensive Sanctification Model" is step 3. This is important to note. The ISM is one tool that is available as part of the larger process. The ISM has three phases. The order matters; we begin with truth.

ISM-Truth: Revealing What Needs to Be Healed or Removed

Jesus said, "You will know the truth, and the truth will set you free" (John 8:32). As pastor Glenn Dorsey once said, "It's not the truth that sets me free; it's the truth that I know which does it."[2] Inner healing begins when hidden things are exposed in a safe, Spirit-led environment. Through guided questions and biblical reflection, individuals can identify emotional wounds, spiritual compromise, or sinful patterns that have kept them bound.

2. Dorsey, *Out of the Snare*.

The Hebrews 12 Assessment

Hebrews 12:14–17 outlines a pathway that leads away from intimacy with God:

> Strive for peace with everyone, and for the holiness without which no one will see the Lord. See to it that no one fails to obtain the grace of God; that no "root of bitterness" springs up and causes trouble, and by it many become defiled; that no one is sexually immoral or unholy like Esau, who sold his birthright for a single meal. For you know that afterward, when he desired to inherit the blessing, he was rejected, for he found no chance to repent, though he sought it with tears (Heb 12:14–17).

Beginning with the admonition to strive for peace with everyone, each phrase represents a successive stage in the journey away from peace with God and others. When we stop living at peace with others, it impacts our holiness. When we compromise our holiness, it damages our view of and relationship with God. Once our relationship with God is impacted, we are in danger of stepping outside his grace. This is when the roots of bitterness set in, and trouble overwhelms us. The next stage is personal defilement, or a sense of uncleanness. When someone feels unclean, they may be more likely to commit sexual sin or to entertain unholy thoughts. Carnal appetites take over, and tragically, the things that matter most are sacrificed. This all results in the absence of God's blessing and acceptance, and the result is a tormented state that is filled with regret.

Ask each of the following questions. Do not send this paper home with people to fill out. That misses the point. The ISM-Truth is not a set of intake questions. It is an invitation to dialogue that can break spiritual strongholds. Ask each question, paying close attention to body language as well as to what the person says, and listening closely to the voice of the Holy Spirit throughout this conversation:

1. Is there anyone that you are currently not at peace with? How are your relationships?
2. Are you living a holy life? If you were going to see God today, what changes would you want to make first?
3. Is there an area of life where you feel an absence of God's grace? Are there any nagging sins or situations that you cannot seem to get victory over?

4. Are there any roots of bitterness in your life? With whom do you feel angry or resentful?
5. Is there anything you feel troubled by?

Pause for a second. Questions 4 and 5 are vital. This is the stage where the conversations we've had about trauma throughout this book become important. When you ask these questions, zero in on the question of trauma. Multitudes of people remain troubled by things that happened ten, twenty, or even fifty years ago. Another way to ask this might be, "Have you been through anything in life that still bothers you to this day?" Be gentle, but this is the place to ask questions about abuse, neglect, and betrayal. Don't let this become overly clinical. People are entrusting you with information that they may have never shared with anyone. I often find that this is the place where breakthrough begins. Let's continue.

6. Defilement is a synonym for uncleanness. When someone was "unclean" in biblical times, they were temporarily separated from God's house, his people, and his presence. Are you struggling in any of those three arenas? Do you faithfully gather in the house of God? How is your relationship with the people of God? Are you consistent in prayer and worship, and do you sense God's presence in your life? If the answer to any of these is no, why do you think that is?
7. Have you committed sexual sins or done things you consider unholy?
8. Do you feel driven by lust or other appetites?
9. Are there any areas where you feel a lack of God's blessing or acceptance?
10. Overall, are you satisfied with your life? Do you have any major regrets?

The Mark 7 Assessment

Depending on the circumstance, a minister might use one of these biblical assessments instead of the other. It is not necessary to use both Mark 7 and Hebrews 12 in every intensive sanctification session, as there is some definite overlap between the two. However, they do work together to help people get a thorough image of themselves and what may unconsciously impact their relationship with God.

Jesus said that people are defiled by the things that come out of their hearts. Given the Gospel of Mark's consistent use of Levitical clean/unclean language, it is likely that he intends to portray Jesus as saying that these things can create an unclean state that isolates people from God's presence, his house, and his people. Ask the following questions, paying close attention to the person's non-verbal cues and to the voice of the Holy Spirit:

1. Do you find yourself dwelling on evil thoughts? If so, what are they? Is there a pattern to them?
2. Have you committed sexual sin? Is there any kind of ongoing sexual sin in your life? Pornography? Fornication? Sexual addiction?
3. Have you ever stolen anything? If so, did you take steps to make amends? This may extend beyond material items. Have you taken credit for something you did not actually do? Have you stolen God's glory in some way? Are you faithful in tithes and offerings?
4. Have you murdered anyone? Jesus said that if you are angry at someone without a cause, it is like murder (Matt 5:22). Is there anyone you are harboring anger toward?
5. Have you violated your marriage vows or someone else's? Have you harbored lust in your heart?
6. Are you guilty of covetousness? That is, do you regularly crave things that are not rightly yours?
7. Have you acted wickedly or in a way that you know is against God's law?
8. Have you deceived anyone? Are there any areas where you are being dishonest with yourself?
9. Do you act or speak in a sensual manner outside the boundaries of marriage?
10. Are you envious of anyone?
11. Have you slandered anyone? Do you use your words to tear others down?
12. Are you prideful? Do you find yourself boasting about your accomplishments or trying to "one up" others?
13. Are you guilty of foolishness? Do you get so caught up in lightheartedness that it becomes hurtful to others? Do you neglect things that need to be done because you are obsessed with entertainment?

Occult Activity Assessment

Although occult activity is not mentioned in Hebrews 12 or Mark 7, the Old and New Testament both have much to say about it (Deut 18:10–14; Is 8:19; Gal 5:18–21; Rev 22:15). Further, Acts 19:11–20 documents the successful deliverance ministry of the Apostle Paul, the failed attempt of the traveling exorcists to invoke the name of Christ like a magical formula, and the burning of occult books as part of the gospel's triumph over dark powers. As noted throughout this book, modern day deliverance ministries also consistently caution against occult involvement. It is therefore reasonable to ask people who are seeking freedom if they have past or present involvement in witchcraft and/or other aspects of the occult.

I recommend using the Occult Activity Assessment in addition to one of the other two assessments. Ask the following questions, paying close attention to the person's body language and to the Holy Spirit's voice:

1. Do you practice any form of witchcraft, or have you done so in the past?
2. Have you made any kind of covenants or pacts that might be considered ungodly?
3. Have you attempted to gain information by communicating with spirits or with those who are deceased?
4. Have you tried to influence others using any kind of paranormal abilities or spells?
5. Have you engaged in any other kinds of occult activities that you feel should be mentioned?

Any "yes" answers must be followed by specific repentance and renunciation through the Name of Christ.

ISM-Blood: Applying the Cleansing Power of Christ

The dialogue that happens while walking through the ISM-Truth serves two vital roles:

1. It breaks the chains of silence and secrecy, which often results in immediate spiritual breakthrough.
2. It guides us as we appropriate the cleansing power of Christ's blood through prayer.

1 John 1:7, 9 reminds us that the blood of Jesus cleanses us from all sin as we confess. Walk with the person through each revealed issue:

- Lead them to *repent* of each sin aloud, being as specific as possible.
- Lead them to *renounce* their involvement with the specific issue and ask God to break its power. If there is a noticeable sense of spiritual heaviness or darkness surrounding the struggle, guide them to also renounce any spiritual influence connected to it. While scholars may differ on whether demons can be accurately named as "spirits of anger," "lust," or "fear," there is broad agreement that demonic powers often harass or tempt people in these specific areas. In this moment, naming the spirit is not about uncovering its proper name—it's about identifying its function and proclaiming Christ's victory over that part of the person's life.
- Allow time for *forgiveness*, both receiving and giving.

If the issue is *trauma*, shift toward healing prayer:

- Invite the person to share their story. When someone shares a traumatic experience, talk to them about how they felt in that moment. Ask what changed in their life, emotions, or relationships in that season. In multiple Gospel accounts, we see mute spirits being cast out—suggesting that the enemy often seeks to silence those he oppresses. If possession results in total silence, it stands to reason that oppression may involve a gradual loss of voice. Trauma, too, has a way of stealing a person's ability to speak freely. Let this time of prayer be an opportunity to help restore their voice, offering them a safe space to speak truth and begin healing.
- Pause at significant moments to pray. Say things like, "God I thank you that you were present even when he/she couldn't see you. They often felt alone and forsaken, but we are thankful that your grace and love brought them to this moment so that they can experience your healing and freedom."
- Ask the Holy Spirit to reveal Jesus in their pain and boldly ask him to work miracles in that moment.

Be tender. Be Spirit-sensitive. This is sacred ground. As you pray, acknowledge the weight and wonder of this moment. Invite the cleansing power of Christ with words like, "Lord Jesus, let Your precious blood wash away every sin and break every stronghold. Thank You that Your sacrifice is enough, and Your grace is sufficient."

ISM-Holy Spirit: Inviting His Presence and Power

The Holy Spirit is the Deliverer. He searches hearts, exposes what is hidden, and brings supernatural peace. Throughout the ISM process, remain attuned to his whisper. Welcome his presence into the room, and gently encourage the person to receive him fully and personally.

In many deliverance sessions, there comes a sacred moment when the Holy Spirit moves in unmistakable power. As you walk together through truth, repentance, renunciation, and faith in the blood of Jesus, prepare your own heart—and theirs—for a holy in-breaking of his freedom. Be expectant. Be reverent. He is faithful to come.

If demonic manifestation arises:

- Command silence (Mark 1:25).
- Do not argue with spirits or seek information from them.
- Be Spirit-led in your prayers and with your words to the individual.
- Return to repentance if necessary.
- Command them to leave in the name of Jesus.
- Don't settle for anything less than complete deliverance.
- After the demon leaves, ask the Holy Spirit to fill the individual with peace and declare God's blessing over their life.
- Lead them in a prayer of total surrender to Jesus Christ and take time to worship, thanking God for the freedom he has given.

The goal is not just freedom *from* something; it is intimacy *with* Someone—Christ. Deliverance is a process, not a performance. Let the Spirit lead. Let Jesus be glorified, and let every captive be set free.

Final Reflections for Pastors

- Every situation is unique. There is no "one size fits all" approach to deliverance ministry. At times, one model may offer the best fit. During other moments, you may feel led to borrow various elements from the approaches discussed throughout this book, and there will undoubtedly be times when the Spirit directs you to go entirely off script. Nonetheless, familiarity with each model equips pastors to respond wisely.

- Deliverance is not just a moment of expulsion. It is a journey of restoration.
- The most successful deliverance is accompanied by the renewing of the mind, the embrace of spiritual identity, and the love of a healing community.

Let's be people who understand both the power of God and the pain of the people we serve. Let us not be hasty to label, nor hesitant to confront darkness. May we walk in discernment, humility, and the authority Christ has given his church. This is the harmonized path of liberation and integration. This is the heartbeat of *The Deliverance Dialogues*.

Questions to Discuss

1. Why is it important that deliverance begins with the Lordship of Jesus rather than with directly confronting demonic powers?
2. The chapter emphasizes that the goal is not merely to expel darkness but to lead people into the light of Christ. How can the church ensure that deliverance ministry is more than just casting out spirits, but also guiding people into the ongoing light, healing, and discipleship of Christ?
3. Why is it important to integrate all three—truth, Christ's blood, and the Holy Spirit—in deliverance ministry, and what happens when one of these dimensions is neglected?
4. The Hebrews 12 and Mark 7 assessments involve deep, probing questions that may surface painful memories or trauma. How can pastors and leaders create safe spaces for people to process painful memories or trauma that surface during deliverance, while still pressing into the freedom Christ offers?
5. The chapter warns against treating deliverance like a "performance" and stresses the importance of walking with people beyond the moment. What practical steps can we take to walk with people after a deliverance moment, ensuring long-term growth and integration rather than a one-time emotional experience?

Conclusion

The Dragon and the Deliverer

In C. S. Lewis's *The Voyage of the Dawn Treader*, a self-absorbed boy named Eustace Clarence Scrubb is transformed into a dragon. "Sleeping on a dragon's hoard with greedy, dragonish thoughts in his heart, he had become a dragon himself," Lewis writes.[1] In this haunting scene, the boy's inward corruption becomes an outward reality, one that isolates him from the people he loves and distorts his desires.[2] Though he tries in vain to peel off his dragon skin, he cannot free himself. True deliverance comes only when he surrenders to Aslan—the great lion, the Christ-figure—who tears through his scaly flesh, throws him into a purifying pool, and restores his true identity.[3]

So it is with those suffering under the weight of demonization. Some have spent years imprisoned by torment, their sense of self twisted by trauma, sin, or spiritual deception. Many have tried every means of relief—therapy, medication, self-help, even religion—only to discover that the "dragon skin" won't come off. Others have been misunderstood, misdiagnosed, or mistreated, left to suffer in silence or isolation. But there is a Lion. His name is Jesus.[4] He has the authority to remove what no human hand can reach.

1. Lewis, *Chronicles of Narnia*, 670.

2. Lewis, *Chronicles of Narnia*, 671.

3. Lewis, *Chronicles of Narnia*, 672.

4. Lewis, *Chronicles of Narnia*, 779. At the conclusion of *The Voyage of the Dawn Treader*, the children are devastated to learn that some of them will not return to Narnia. Aslan responds, "But there I have another name. You must learn to know me by that name." This is a beautiful picture of the reality of Christ, the Lion of the tribe of Judah.

Throughout this book, we've traced a theological, clinical, and pastoral path through the shadowy terrain of demonization, mental illness, and spiritual healing. Along the way, important patterns have emerged. Preternatural signs matter, but they are not always present, which means that discerning between severe demonization and certain dissociative disorders can be profoundly difficult. Yet across cultures and religions—from a young woman in Pakistan to a Southern Baptist man in the United States—the symptoms of possession share a remarkable consistency. What divides professionals and ministers is not usually the question of whether these phenomena exist, but how they are best addressed. Again and again, the most hopeful outcomes rise from integrative approaches—models where pastoral authority and spiritual discernment are held in tension with clinical wisdom and therapeutic care, rather than pitted against them.

The Pentecostal and Charismatic movements have been torchbearers of deliverance and healing for over a century.[5] The task before us is to carry it with greater humility, wisdom, and partnership than ever before. This is not a time for retreat into dogma or suspicion of science. It is a moment to step boldly into dialogue—pastors, clinicians, physicians, and trauma-informed caregivers working side by side for the healing of the whole person. When such a table is set, powerful things happen.

The Deliverance Dialogues is more than a book; it is a summons. We stand at a cultural crossroads. Paganism rises. Mental anguish spreads. Spiritual darkness tightens its grip. But we are not left powerless. We have the gospel. We have the Spirit. We have the Name above every name. We have a sword, the Word of God, that summons a power greater than that of Grayskull. This is no myth. This is no fantasy. This is the power of the living Christ.

Pastors, counselors, and believers alike—this is your moment. Step into the dialogue. Reclaim your voice, and let the world know that deliverance

5. York, *Missions in the Age of the Spirit*, 206; See also McGee, *People of the Spirit*, chap 1; Oliver, *Pentecost to the Present*, 260; Seymour, "Testimonies of Healing," 6. McGee notes that throughout the early 1900's, Pentecostals were viewed as "absurd and irresponsible," because their opponents did not foresee "the impact that healings and 'power encounters' (exorcisms, etc.) would have in capturing the attention of non-Christians on the mission fields." Missiologist John York writes, "When demonic manifestations occur, pastors or trained lay leaders deal immediately with the people who are affected. The testimonies of those delivered from sickness and demonic attack give great credibility to the preaching of the gospel, much as they did during the New Testament era. . . . [M]inistries of healing and deliverance from demons are typical of Pentecostal church planting throughout the world."

is not a relic of the past but the living ministry of Jesus Christ for today. If we—the church, the Body of Christ—will rise to the occasion with humility, wisdom, and Spirit-empowered compassion, then perhaps those who are suffering will echo Eustace's confession: *"I'd turned into a boy again."*[6]

Restored. Redeemed. Delivered.

6. Lewis, *Chronicles of Narnia*, 682.

Appendix A

The Importance of Forming Therapeutic Alliances

IN SPIRITUAL WARFARE AND deliverance ministry, one of the most overlooked tools in the arsenal of the church is relationship. Not only is relationship with the afflicted vital—but also relationship between pastors and mental health professionals, between churches and recovery ministries, and between intercessors and clinicians.

In this appendix, I want to explore why therapeutic alliances are not a compromise of our convictions, but a confirmation of our calling to bring holistic healing to the people God entrusts to our care.

Theological and Clinical Integration is Not a Threat—It's a Strategy

Psychiatrist M. Scott Peck once wrote, "Psychology and theology are so integrated as to be interdependent branches of the same science."[1] While that's not the consensus across either discipline, it reflects a powerful truth: people are multifaceted beings, and effective ministry must address both spiritual and psychological dimensions.

In the doctoral project that formed the basis for this book, pastors initially demonstrated confidence in theological categories but less confidence

1. Peck, *Glimpses of the Devil*, 1.

when it came to helping people in practical ways—especially in distinguishing between mental illness and demonization. Thankfully, we don't have to possess every gift, skill, or professional qualification as long as we are willing to collaborate with others. My research yielded an encouraging revelation: Even without formal training, many pastors already possessed a willingness to form therapeutic alliances. That posture is vital. It's what opens the door for practical, Spirit-led collaboration.[2]

Why Pastors Need Mental Health Partners

The need for therapeutic partnerships becomes obvious when we acknowledge the complexity of human distress. A person's suffering may stem from personal sin, spiritual bondage, childhood trauma, neurological dysfunction, or any combination of the above. It is unlikely that one person will be an expert on all of this.

That's why the early church functioned as a body—different members with different gifts working together in unity (1 Cor 12). Today, the church needs Spirit-empowered pastors and well-trained therapists to join forces. We need alliances that honor the sanctity of Scripture while embracing the insights of science.

When pastors dismiss clinical input, we risk misdiagnosing illness as possession—or worse, subjecting traumatized people to harmful forms of ministry. When therapists dismiss spiritual realities, they risk leaving clients unhealed and spiritually vulnerable. The truth is—we need each other.

Best Practices for Healthy Collaboration

Here are several recommendations drawn from my research that can help churches form strong therapeutic alliances:

1. **Establish Clear Referral Pathways**

   Pastors should never attempt to diagnose mental illness or discourage someone from taking prescribed medication. If supernatural signs are not clearly present, a referral for mental and physical evaluation should be standard protocol.[3]

2. Willis, "Liberation and Integration," 133.
3. Willis, "Liberation and Integration," 145–48.

2. **Create Informed Consent Processes**

   Before engaging in deliverance ministry or emotional healing, individuals should sign a waiver that explains the nature of the intervention and the qualifications of the minister. This establishes clarity and trust among all parties.[4]

3. **Partner with Christian Mental Health Professionals**

   Seek out counselors and doctors who acknowledge the spiritual dimension of healing. While they may not share your theology in full, their openness to dialogue makes true partnership possible.[5]

4. **Offer Training that Emphasizes Teamwork**

   Regional seminars and local church workshops should be designed with both ministers and clinicians in mind—training that brings both communities to the table fosters shared language and mutual respect.

5. **Recognize the Value of Story**

   Therapeutic alliances flourish when ministry leaders listen well. Whether in prayer sessions or counseling rooms, trust grows as we help people find healing in the context of their story. Relational safety is often the first key to freedom.

Therapeutic Exorcism and Shared Authority

Dennis Bull's model of "therapeutic exorcism" reflects this idea beautifully. His approach calls pastors and therapists to collaborate with afflicted individuals rather than dominating them. He insists that the person should feel empowered to take part in their own liberation and healing.[6] This honors both personal agency and spiritual authority.

Therapeutic alliances are not about merging professions. They are about honoring distinct roles while pursuing a shared goal: the holistic healing of the human soul.

4. Willis, "Liberation and Integration," 147.
5. Willis, "Liberation and Integration," 146, 263–64.
6. Bull, "Phenomenological Model," 131–36.

A Call to the Church

The church must not act as if deliverance ministry and mental health care are rivals. The enemy's greatest tactic is to divide the very forces that could work together to destroy his grip on people's lives. We must train altar workers to collaborate with trauma-informed counselors. We must equip pastors to make wise referrals. We must empower therapists to welcome spiritual realities into their work. Most importantly, we must pray for humble hearts and unified teams so that those who are bound can find freedom, not only in Christ's name, but in Christ's people.

Appendix B

Ethics in Deliverance Ministry

Deliverance ministry is not just a spiritual undertaking—it is a deeply ethical one. The weight of responsibility on those who confront demonic influence cannot be overstated. How we minister—our posture, tone, and method—matters just as much as our theology. Ethical deliverance protects the dignity of the afflicted, honors the power of the Holy Spirit, and guards against harm that can result from immature or coercive practices.

In this appendix, we'll explore two especially sensitive topics: speaking to demons and shouting during deliverance. We'll also examine broader ethical boundaries that should guide every minister who steps into this sacred work.

Speaking to Demons: Discernment Over Drama

One of the most hotly debated questions in deliverance ministry is whether it's appropriate to speak directly to demons. Some practitioners regularly engage demons in extended dialogue. Others refuse to allow any expression from the enemy at all.

What does Scripture show us?

In the Gospels, Jesus only asked for a demon's name once (Mark 5:9; Luke 8:30). In other instances, he refused to permit the demons to speak (Mark 1:34; Luke 4:35, 41). These examples suggest that while limited engagement is occasionally warranted, prolonged conversation with demons is not modeled by Christ.

The goal is not to gain information from demons but to expel them in the name of Jesus. It is noteworthy that Jesus never used information gained from a demon to cast it out. It is true that in the case of the man with the legion, Jesus asked for its name. Notably, however, he did not use that name when driving it out. Demons are deceivers by nature. Trusting their words places us on dangerous ground. Any communication should be minimal, Spirit-led, and purposeful.

Should Ministers Shout? Power Flows from Authority, Not from Volume

Pentecostal traditions are often known for passionate prayer. In many contexts, spiritual intensity is accompanied by raised voices, dramatic gestures, or forceful declarations. While there is certainly biblical precedent for fervent prayer (Jas 5:16), we must be careful not to confuse spiritual authority with emotional intensity.

This distinction is especially important in situations involving trauma or dissociation. People experiencing dissociative episodes—particularly those with dissociative identity disorder—may react negatively to loud or forceful ministry. In fact, shouting may intensify their distress or compound previous trauma.[1]

It is my personal tendency to preach and pray loudly, but let's be clear: Faith does not require volume. Jesus cast out demons with a word. His authority was not measured in decibels. For pastors and lay ministers alike, calm, Spirit-led direction often carries more weight than aggressive theatrics.

Coercion Has No Place in Deliverance

One of the gravest ethical errors in deliverance ministry is the use of coercion. This includes:

- Forcing someone to undergo deliverance when they are not willing.
- Pressuring people to stop medications without medical supervision.

1. Willis, "Liberation and Integration," 260–61.

- Assuming that every distress is demonic and pushing a narrative that doesn't match their reality.
- Using fear tactics to force confessions or decisions.

Psychologist Dennis Bull observes that exorcisms can be experienced as "revictimization" when done "to" the patient rather than "*with*" the patient.[2] Deliverance must always honor the person's agency, inviting them to participate in their own healing journey. Gentleness, consent, and collaboration are essential.

Jesus Is Our Model—Not the Manifestation

It can be easy to fall into the trap of chasing manifestations—seeking the spectacle of spiritual warfare instead of the heart of Christ. However, the Gospels remind us that Jesus never made a show of deliverance. In fact, he warned people not to trust in signs alone (Matt 12:39). His goal was always restoration, not drama.

As ministers, our job is not to draw attention to ourselves or to the demons, but to point people to Jesus, helping them find wholeness, dignity, and peace.

Ethical Guardrails for Ministers

The following guidelines should be considered essential for any ethical deliverance practice:

1. **Do not diagnose mental illness or advise people to stop medication.** That is outside the scope of pastoral authority and can have deadly consequences.[3]
2. **Only engage in deliberate deliverance ministry with appropriate oversight.** This includes informed consent and approval from church leadership.[4]
3. **Avoid ministering alone.** Whenever possible, include a second trained individual to ensure accountability and safety.

2. Bull, "Phenomenological Model," 132–34.
3. Willis, "Liberation and Integration," 146.
4. Willis, "Liberation and Integration," 146–48.

4. **Be trauma-informed.** Learn the signs of dissociation, PTSD, and other common responses to trauma so that you do not mislabel or mistreat suffering individuals.
5. **Reject theatrics.** Deliverance is not performance. The goal is not entertainment, but restoration.
6. **Always seek the guidance of the Holy Spirit.** No technique or formula can replace the discernment that comes from God.

In Summary

Deliverance ministry must be Spirit-empowered, Scripture-informed, and ethically grounded. It is not a place for manipulation, theatrics, or bravado. It is a sacred space where broken people encounter the liberating power of Jesus Christ. Let us minister with confidence—but let us also minister with compassion, humility, and care.

The kingdom of God is not built through volume or confrontation but through the authority of Jesus, expressed in love and led by the Spirit.

Appendix C

Demonization and Believers

A KEY GOAL OF this book is to equip pastors to help people who are distressed by demonic influence or mental illness. Although pastors are at times called upon to offer help to those outside the church, much of their focus is naturally on ministry to those who identify as followers of Christ. Therefore, it is reasonable for readers to concern themselves with what kinds of distress may be encountered among believers.[1]

1. I originally wrote Appendix C as part of my doctoral work at AGTS because I realized that those reading my research and findings might naturally wonder what conclusions I draw regarding demonization and believers. This is often a polarizing issue, with strong feelings naturally arising on all sides. Some people fear that claims of demonization among believers increase the likelihood of mental and physical illnesses going untreated. Further, it is sometimes asserted that belief in demonization among believers undermines the integrity of the New Testament's teaching on soteriology (the doctrine of salvation) and shirks human responsibility for sinful decisions, illegitimately transferring blame to demons. These are valid concerns. At the same time, others fear that people who desperately need spiritual deliverance may not receive the ministry they need if demonization is not considered as a possible root of their distress. This is also a valid concern. The matter is further complicated by differences in understanding of the believer's security among people from various faith traditions. The Assemblies of God's position paper that can be accessed at https://ag.org/Beliefs/Position-Papers/Spiritual-Warfare-and-the-Believer offers excellent insight on this subject as well. While this appendix may not account for every theological nuance that is relevant to this conversation, it is intended to offer helpful pastoral guidance as part of the larger body of research that is presented throughout this book.

It is common for authors who, like me, are writing from a Pentecostal perspective to assert that Christians cannot be demon possessed. I agree with this assertion. However, valid concerns could be raised about whether those who hold to this theological position may fail to account for the broad spectrum of demonic attacks. The Assemblies of God's Position Paper on Spiritual Warfare and the Believer offers significant insight:

> The conflict between the believer and demonic forces can be understood as a spectrum of demonic influence, ranging in the degree of domination over a person's life and in the variety of aspects of life where demonic control has taken place. The impact of demonic powers may be slight and almost undetectable. If one repents, forsakes their sin and carnal activities, resists temptation, and calls upon the Spirit to cleanse and deliver, victory and freedom will be obtained. The extreme influence of the demonic could be called "possession" in which a person is controlled by demonic forces who manipulate the individual's body, mind, and spirit for their destructive purposes. This extreme case of demonic control is indicative of continued movement away from, and abandonment of, a personal relationship with Jesus; the believer should gain victory in the spiritual conflict well before this extreme and not be subject to it. While believers will engage in spiritual warfare and will be oppressed, they cannot be possessed by the demonic forces.[2]

This well-articulated summary of a classic Pentecostal position provides an excellent starting point for understanding the complex nature of this conversation.

The word "possession" has been used throughout this book to reference the most severe forms of demonization. It also appears in the psychological literature that I reviewed as part of my dissertation to explain various mental health conditions in which individuals feel that they are under the control of a spirit.[3] However, it is important to note that there has been a strong shift away from using the word "possession" in theological writings on this subject. Michael Heiser effectively frames the discussion:

2. Assemblies of God General Presbytery, "Spiritual Warfare and the Believer." The following footnote is included as part of this paragraph in the position paper: "With demon possession, the power of Satan takes control of the center of an individual's personality. In such lives, demons can manifest themselves through temporary changes in personality, speech, bizarre physical behavior, physical and mental affliction, and self-destructive tendencies."

3. Willis, "Liberation and Integration," chap 3.

> Can a Christian be demon possessed? Christian writers have taken both sides of this issue. The disagreement in part derives from semantics, but that is not to imply that the debate lacks substance. The semantic problem derives from English translations of the Greek lemmas in passages describing demonized individuals. Words like "possess" and "possession" denote ownership. A close reading of the New Testament ought to make it clear that a member of the body of Christ cannot be owned by Satan or demons.[4]

However, this begs the question of whether the New Testament authors intended to convey the idea of demonic ownership in demon possession. Heiser explains, "No Greek word for "possession" or "ownership" appears in passages to clarify or define the activity described by *daimonizomai*. It is English semantics, not the Greek lemma, which have led to the controversy over whether Christians can be possessed by demons."[5]

Although I concur with Heiser's analysis of New Testament possession language, his expanded explanation of demonization falls short of settling the issue as it relates to deliverance ministry. Heiser continues,

> On this the New Testament is clear, as several passages employ language that suggests Christians can fall under the influence of Satan and evil spirits. Paul warned Timothy about certain teachers in this regard: "Now the Spirit expressly says that in later times some will depart from the faith by devoting themselves to deceitful spirits and teachings of demons" (1 Tim 4:1). That those doing so were "departing from the faith" indicates that those Paul had in view were professing believers. For sure, these false teachers did not see what they were doing as out of step with the faith. . . . In his second letter to Timothy, Paul's language was even more foreboding, instructing Timothy to gently correct such opponents so they might "escape from the snare of the devil, after being captured by him to do his will" (2 Tim 2:26). The idea that believers could be captured by Satan and made servants of his will certainly fits the notion of demonization, though it lacks the bizarre physical torment of episodes in the Gospels.[6]

Heiser's observations are deeply significant. However, this explanation of demonization fails to account for some of the key issues. The absence of "the bizarre physical torment of episodes in the Gospels" significantly

4. Heiser, *Demons*, 253.
5. Heiser, *Demons*, 254.
6. Heiser, *Demons*, 255–56.

distinguishes the passages here referenced by Heiser from the exorcism accounts of the Gospels.[7]

Many Pentecostals readily acknowledge that believers need to guard themselves against deception and that repentance from sin is imperative, but this is hardly the same as the gospel accounts of those whose minds or bodies were overtaken by malicious forces and could only be liberated by divine intervention. I agree with Heiser that the language of demonization is helpful for explaining the spectrum of diabolic attacks. Nonetheless, the substance of the gospel accounts makes it clear that some forms of demonization can be so severe that the human personality is overtaken. The debate surrounding deliverance ministry with Christians is decidedly focused on this aspect of demonization.

Nothing in the New Testament implies that born-again Christians should fear having their minds or bodies casually overtaken by demons. However, the teaching of the Bible and of the Assemblies of God is that habitual sin can have devastating consequences and may result in believers forfeiting divine protection. Stated another way, individuals may attend our local churches who profess faith in Christ but who are, from a Pentecostal perspective, backslidden. This has significant pastoral implications.

Although it is reasonable to assume that those who abide in Christ are protected from extreme demonization, many factors may exist in the lives of churchgoers of which their pastor is not aware. The primary context of this project focuses on a pastoral counseling setting and assumes that those seeking help are experiencing some kind of spiritual or psychological distress. Within that context, a thorough evaluation of what led the person to seek help is warranted. The Assemblies of God Position Paper offers this wisdom:

> Great care must be taken not to confuse emotional and mental illnesses with demonic activity. While the demonic activity may mimic the behavior exhibited in mental illness, to assert that they are the same can bring harm to individuals, preventing them from receiving the medical care needed. The wise counsel of godly doctors, counselors, and psychologists can be of assistance in discerning the actual condition. The powerful and all-wise Holy Spirit provides discernment and wisdom to those who minister to humans facing this severe challenge.[8]

7. Heiser, *Demons*, 255–56

8. Assemblies of God General Presbytery, "Spiritual Warfare and the Believer."

There is much wisdom and safety in building therapeutic alliances with other professionals to help in these evaluations.

However, if someone seeking help experiences clear preternatural phenomena and if their struggles are not explained by illness or simple matters of sanctification, due diligence may demand that pastors consider demonization as a potential cause of distress.[9] The pastoral counseling setting provides a natural venue to discuss potential roots of demonization like sin, trauma, and occult activity. Dr. Graham Twelftree insightfully observes, "[W]e should pay as little attention to the demonic as is pastorally possible. Yet we should confront the demonic as much as is pastorally required."[10] Dr. David Lim offers an expansive view of how this may be accomplished,

> Deliverance may be called for that does not require expelling demons, but rather claiming victory over the past with its evil habits and thoughts that put one in bondage. Included in that type of deliverance must be solid Bible teaching, aggressive prayer, control of the thought processes (1 Corinthians 10:4), exercise of the power of God and the will to love (2 Timothy 1:7), Christian counseling, focus on heavenly matters (Colossians 3:1), spiritual growth (Philippians 3:14), support of one another (1 Corinthians 12:26), and surrender of the matter to the glory of God (2 Corinthians 12:7). . .In true cases of demonic possession, a person has surrendered his will to demons. . .Those who are possessed project a new personality and voice, experiencing an obliteration of their own personalities for a time. Deliverance is absolutely necessary in these cases.[11]

Pastors should not be quick to assume that someone's distress is demonic in nature. Even when it is, exorcistic approaches should not be the only tools in their pastoral arsenal. Nonetheless, ministers should always remember that the apostolic mandate to preach, heal, and drive out demons is still in force (Matt 10:7–8).

9. The word "preternatural" is closely related to contemporary usage of the word "paranormal." Preternatural activity is a bit more theologically nuanced as opposed to the broad umbrella of paranormal activity. It refers to powers which might be considered natural to an angel or demon but which would not be available to humans under normal circumstances. It is also distinct from "supernatural" activity. In biblical terms, supernatural activity refers to God's intervention in ways that defy natural laws. Throughout this book, I have generally opted to use the language of "paranormal activity" since it is likely more familiar to many of today's readers.

10. Twelftree, *In the Name of Jesus*, 294.

11. Lim. *Spiritual Gifts*, 84.

About The Author

Dr. Robbie Willis and his wife, Anna May, serve as Discipleship Pastors with Link Church. They have been blessed with eight children. Although two of them have already gone home to be with Christ, the other six continue to fill their lives with joy, along with their daughter-in-law and their grandson, Judah.

Robbie holds a Bachelor of Arts from Central Bible College. He also earned a Master of Arts and a Doctor of Ministry in Spiritual Formation from Assemblies of God Theological Seminary (AGTS). In addition to his role at Link Church, Robbie serves as an adjunct professor with AGTS's Doctor of Ministry program and with Global University's Graduate School of Theology.

Sources Consulted

Allen, Thomas B. *Possessed: The True Story of an Exorcism*. Lincoln, NE: iUniverse.com, 2000.

American Psychiatric Association. *Diagnostic and Statistical Manual of Mental Disorders 2022 [TR] DSM 5*. Washington, DC: APAP, 2022.

Amorth, Gabriele. *An Exorcist Explains the Demonic: The Antics of Satan and His Army of Fallen Angels*. Manchester, NH: Sophia, 2016.

———. *An Exorcist Tells His Story*. San Francisco: Ignatius, 2015.

Annacondia, Carlos. *Listen to Me Satan: Keys for Breaking the Devil's Grip and Bringing Revival to Your World*. Lake Mary, FL: Charisma House, 2008.

Anderson, Neal T. *The Bondage Breaker: Overcoming Negative Thoughts, Irrational Feelings, and Habitual Sins*. Irvine, CA: Harvest House, 2019.

Annus, Amar. "On the Origin of the Watchers: A Comparative Study of the Antediluvian Wisdom in Mesopotamian and Jewish Traditions." *Journal for the Study of the Pseudepigrapha* 19(4) (2010) 277– 320.

Appleby, David. "Deliverance as Part of the Therapeutic Process." In *Transformative Encounters: The Intervention of God in Christian Counseling and Pastoral Care*, edited by David Appleby and George Ohlschlager, 77–93. Lisle, IL: IVP Academic, 2013.

———. *It's Only a Demon: A Model of Christian Deliverance*. 2nd ed. Goode, VA: Spiritual Interventions, 2017.

Assemblies of God General Presbytery. "Position Paper: Spiritual Warfare and the Believer." Adopted July 30, 2019. https://ag.org/Beliefs/Position-Papers/Spiritual-Warfare-and-the-Believer.

Averbeck, Richard E. "דָּוָה (dāwâ), Hebrew GK #1864." In *New International Dictionary of Old Testament Theology & Exegesis*, edited by Willem VanGemeren. Grand Rapids, MI: Zondervan, 1997.

Bagglio, Matt. *The Rite: The Making of a Modern Exorcist*. New York: Destiny Image, 2010.

Baoloian, Bruce. "שָׂטָן (śāṭān), HGK#8477." In *New International Dictionary of Old Testament Theology & Exegesis*, edited by Willem VanGemeren. Grand Rapids, MI: Zondervan, 1997.

Barry, Alyson M. "A Qualitative Analysis of Reports of Dissociative Trance Experiences in the United States." PhD diss., Seattle Pacific University, 2012. ProQuest.

Sources Consulted

Basu, Soumya, Subhash C. Gupta, and Sayeed Akthar. "Trance and Possession Like Symptoms in a Case of CNS Lesion: A Case Report." *Indian Journal of Psychiatry* 44(1) (2002) 65–67.

Bauckham, Richard. *Jesus and the Eyewitnesses: The Gospels as Eyewitness Testimony.* Grand Rapids, MI: Eerdmans, 2006. Kindle.

Bauer, Nicole M. "The Devil and the Doctor: The (De)Medicalization of Exorcism in the Roman Catholic Church." *Religions* 13(2) (Feb 2022) 1–13.

Bauer, Nicole M., and Andrew J. Doole. "The (Re)Invention of Biblical Exorcism in Contemporary Roman Catholic Discourses." *Religion and Theology* 29(1–2) (2022) 1–33.

Bennet, Robert H. *I Am Not Afraid: Demon Possession and Spiritual Warfare.* Concordia, 2013.

Bhavsar, Vishal, Antonio Ventriglio, and Dinesh Bhugra. "Dissociative Trance and Spirit Possession: Challenges for Cultures in Transition." *Psychiatry and Clinical Neurosciences* 70(12) (December 2016) 551–59.

Bilu, Yoram. "The Taming of the Deviants and Beyond: An Analysis of Dybbuk Possession and Exorcism in Judaism." *The Psychoanalytic Study of Society* (2019) 1–32. Routledge.

Bondo, Mayuka G., and Marius Nel. "Charismatic Experiences in the Congo Evangelistic Mission Churches: A Review of Some Practices." *In Die Skriflig In Luce Verbi* 56(1) (2022) 1–8.

Boring, M. Eugene. *Mark: A Commentary.* Louisville, KY: Westminster John Knox, 2006. Kindle.

Bottari, Pablo. *Free in Christ: Your Complete Handbook on the Ministry of Deliverance.* Lake Mary, FL: Charisma House, 2000.

Bottoms, B. L., et al. "In the Name of God: A Profile of Religion-Related Child Abuse." *Journal of Social Issues* 51(2) (1995) 85–111.

Bourguignon, Erika. "Hallucination and Trance: An Anthropologist's Perspective." In *Origin and Mechanisms of Hallucinations: Proceedings of the 14th Annual Meeting of the Eastern Psychiatric Research Association held in New York City, November 14–15, 1969*, 183–90. Boston: Springer US, 1970.

———. *Possession.* San Francisco: Chandler and Sharp, 1976.

Bradnick, David L. *Evil, Spirits and Possession: An Emergentist Theology of the Demonic.* Global Pentecostal and Charismatic Studies 25. Boston, MA: Brill, 2017.

Bull, Dennis L. "A Phenomenological Model of Therapeutic Exorcism for Dissociative Identity Disorder." *Journal of Psychology & Theology* 29(2) (2001) 131–39.

Bunta, Silviu N. "Dreamy Angels and Demonic Giants: The Watchers Traditions and the Origin of Evil in Early Christian Demonology." In *The Fallen Angels Traditions: Second Temple Developments and Reception History*, edited by Angela Kim Harkins, Kelley Coblentz Bautch, and John C. Endres, 116–38. Washington, DC: Catholic Biblical Association of America, 2014.

Carl, Jonathan. *Spiritual Warfare in the Early Church: The History of Demonic Activity Among the Ante-Nicene Church Fathers and Beyond.* N.p.: Jonathan Logan Carl, 2022.

Carter, Warren. "Cross-Gendered Romans and Mark's Jesus: Legion Enters the Pigs (Mark 5:1–20)." *Journal of Biblical Literature* 134(1) (2015) 139–55.

Calpino, Teresa. "The Gerasene Demoniac (Mark 5:1–20): The Pre-Markan Function of the Pericope." *Biblical Research* 53 (January 2008) 15–23.

Channabasavanna, S. M., Chandrashekar, C.R., and M. Venkataswamy-Reddy. "Hysterical Possession Syndrome: A Retrospective Study." *Indian Journal of Psychological Medicine* 3(1) (2020) 35–40.

Charles, R. H., trans. *Book of Jubilees.* Oxford: Clarendon, 1913. https://ccel.org/ccel/c/charles/otpseudepig/files/jubilee/index.htm.

Chavez, William S. "Modern Practice, Archaic Ritual: Catholic Exorcism in America." *Religions* 12(10) (2021) 1–27.

Chiang, Jonathan Lee Shoo. *The Importance of Inner Healing and Deliverance for Effective Discipleship.* Wipf & Stock, 2019.

Clark, Randy. *The Biblical Guidebook to Deliverance.* Lake Mary, FL: Charisma House, 2015.

Cuneo, Michael. *American Exorcism: Expelling Demons in the Land of Plenty.* New York: Doubleday, 2001.

De Castro Moreira, Leonardo Vasconcelos. "The Secularisation of Demons: Exorcisms Conducted by the Universal Church of the Kingdom of God in Madrid." *Journal of Contemporary Religion* 37 (1) (2022) 107–24.

Delmonte, Romara, et al. "Can the *DSM-5* Differentiate Between Nonpathological Possession and Dissociative Identity Disorder? A Case Study from an Afro-Brazilian Religion." *Journal of Trauma & Dissociation* 17(3) (2016) 322–37.

De Oliveira Maraldi, Everton, et al. "Cultural Presentations of Dissociation: The Case of Possession Trance Experiences." *Journal of Trauma & Dissociation* 22(1) (2021) 11–16.

Diamond, Stephen. *Anger, Madness, and the Daimonic: The Paradoxical Power of Rage in Violence, Evil, and Creativity.* Plattsburgh: State University of New York Press, 2013.

DiChiara, Alexander. "Dissociation, Possession, Or Otherwise? A Post-Critical Analysis of Exorcism." PhD diss., The Chicago School of Professional Psychology, 2021. ProQuest.

Dorsey, Glenn. *Out of the Snare: A Christian's Guide to Emotional Healing and Deliverance.* Independently Published, 2015.

Driscoll, Mike. "How Catholic Exorcists Distinguish between Demonic Possession and Mental Disorders." PhD diss., Regent University, 2013. ProQuest.

Duijl, Marjolein van, et al. "Dissociative Symptoms and Reported Trauma Among Patients with Spirit Possession and Matched Healthy Controls in Uganda." *Culture, Medicine & Psychiatry* 34(2) (June 2010) 380–400.

Duling, Dennis C. "Solomon, Exorcism, and the Son of David." *Harvard Theological Review* 68(3–4) (Jul– Oct 1975) 235–52.

During, Emmanuel H., et al. "A Critical Review of Dissociative Trance and Possession Disorders: Etiological, Diagnostic, Therapeutic, and Nosological Issues." *The Canadian Journal of Psychiatry* 56(4) (2011) 235–42.

Elder, Nicholas A. "Of Porcine and Polluted Spirits: Reading the Gerasene Demoniac (Mark 5:1–20) with the Book of Watchers (1 Enoch 1–36)." *The Catholic Biblical Quarterly* 78(3) (2016) 430–46.

Forcén, Carlos Espi, and Fernando Espî Forcén. "Demonic Possessions and Mental Illness: Discussion of Selected Cases in Late Medieval Hagiographical Literature." *Early Science & Medicine* 19(3) (2014) 258–79.

Gadit, Amin. "Possession: A Clinical Enigma." *Case Reports* (2011) 1–2.

Gallagher, Richard. *Demonic Foes: My Twenty-Five Years as a Psychiatrist Investigating Possessions, Diabolic Attacks, and the Paranormal.* San Francisco: HarperOne, 2020.

———. "A Case of Demonic Possession." *New Oxford Review* 75(3) (March 2008) 22–32.

———. "True and False Possessions Revisited." *New Oxford Review* 82(4) (May 2015) 22–27.

García Oliva, Javier. "Exorcism and Children: Balancing Protection and Autonomy in the Legal Framework." *International Journal of Law in Context* 18(1) (2022) 55–68.

Garroway, Joshua D. "The Invasion of a Mustard Seed: A Reading of Mark 5.1–20." *Journal for the Study of the New Testament* 32(1) (2009) 57–75.

Gaw, Albert C., et al. "The Clinical Characteristics of Possession Disorder among Twenty Chinese Patients in the Hebei Province of China." *Psychiatric Services* 49(3) (1998) 360–65.

Gee, Donald. *The Fruit of the Spirit*. Springfield, MO: Gospel Publishing House, 1934. Kindle.

Germiniani, Francisco M. B., et al. "Tourette's Syndrome: From Demonic Possession and Psychoanalysis to the Discovery of Gene." *Arquivos de Neuro-Psiquiatria* 70(7) (2012) 547–49.

Gingrich, Heather. *Restoring the Shattered Self: A Christian Counselor's Guide to Complex Trauma*. 2nd ed. Lisle, IL: IVP Academic, 2020

———. *Shattered No More! Healing for Survivors of Abuse, Interpersonal Violence, and Complex Trauma*. Forest, VA: AACC Publishing, 2024.

Girgis, Ragy R. *On Satan, Demons, and Psychiatry: Exploring Mental Illness in the Bible*. Eugene, OR: Wipf and Stock, 2020.

Harkins, Angela Kim. "Elements of the Fallen Angels Traditions in the Qumran Hodayot." In *The Fallen Angels Traditions: Second Temple Developments and Reception History*, edited by Angela Kim Harkins, Kelley Coblentz Bautch, and John C. Endres, 8–24. Washington, DC: Catholic Biblical Association of America, 2014.

Hartley, John E. *Leviticus*. Word Biblical Commentary 4. Grand Rapids, MI: Zondervan, 1992. Kindle.

Hayward, Chris. *God's Cleansing Stream: Developing a Life-Changing Deliverance Ministry in Your Church*. Fort Collins, CO: Arns Publishing, 2020.

Heiser, Michael S. *Demons: What the Bible Really Says About the Powers of Darkness*. Bellingham, WA: Lexham, 2020. Kindle.

———. *Reversing Hermon: Enoch, the Watchers, and the Forgotten Mission of Jesus Christ*. Crane, MO: Defender, 2017. Kindle.

———. *The Unseen Realm: Recovering the Supernatural Worldview of the Bible*. Bellingham, WA: Lexham, 2015.

Hogeterp, Albert L. A. "Trauma and Its Ancient Literary Representation: Mark 5:1–20." *Zeitschrift Für Die Neutestamentliche Wissenschaft Und Die Kunde Der Älteren Kirche* 111(1) (2020) 1–32.

Ibba, Giovanni. "The Evil Spirits in Jubilees and the Spirit of the Bastards in 4Q510 with Some Remarks on Other Qumran Manuscripts." *Henoch* 31(1) (2009) 111– 16.

Isaacs, T. Craig. *In Bondage to Evil: A Psycho-Spiritual Understanding of Possession*. Eugene, OR: Pickwick, 2018.

———. *Revelations and Possession: Distinguishing Spiritual from Psychological Experiences*. Kearney, NE: Morris, 2010.

Januszewski, Gregg A. "The use of Social Constructionist Theory to Inform Treatment Decisions: A Comparison of Dissociative Identity Disorder and Demonic Possession." University of Hartford, 1997.

Johnson, Dave. "Baptism in the Holy Spirit vs Spirit Possession in the Lowland Philippines: Some Considerations for Discipleship." *Asian Journal of Pentecostal Studies: Biblical Responses to Animism in Asia* 21(2) (August 2018) 19–34.

Jung, Carl G., ed. *Man and His Symbols*. New York: Bantam, 1964.

Jöris, Steffen. "The Markan Use of 'Unclean Spirit': Another Messianic Strand." *Australian Biblical Review* 60(1) (2012) 49–66.

Kay, William K., and Robin Parry, eds. *Exorcism and Deliverance: Multi-Disciplinary Studies*. Milton Keynes: Paternoster, 2011.

Keener, Craig S. *Acts: An Exegetical Commentary: 15:1—23:35, Volume 2*. Grand Rapids, MI: Baker Academic, 2014.

———. *Between History and Spirit: The Apostolic Witness of the Book of Acts*. Eugene, OR: Cascade, 2020.

———. *The IVP Background Commentary: New Testament, 2nd Edition*. Downers Grove, IL: Intervarsity, 2014

———. *Miracles: The Credibility of the New Testament Accounts, Volume 2*. Grand Rapids, MI: Baker Academic, 2011.

———. *Spirit Hermeneutics: Reading Scripture in Light of Pentecost*. Grand Rapids, MI: Eerdmans, 2016.

Khalifa, Najat, and Tim Hardie. "Possession and Jinn." *Journal of the Royal Society of Medicine* 98(8) (2005) 351–53.

Khan, I. D., and A. K. Sahni. "Possession Syndrome at High Altitude (4575 m/15000 ft)." *Kathmandu University Medical Journal* 11(3) (2013) 253–55.

Kianpoor, Mohsen, and George F. Rhoades Jr. "Djinnati, A Possession State in Baloochistan, Iran." *Journal of Trauma Practice* (4:1–2) (2006) 147–55.

Kim, Young Kuk. "The Enochic Traditions and Jesus's Exorcism in Mark." PhD diss., Department of New Testament Studies, Dallas Theological Seminary, 2019.

Lee, Jonathan. *The Importance of Inner Healing and Deliverance for Effective Discipleship*. Eugene, OR: Wipf & Stock, 2019.

Lewis, C. S. *The Chronicles of Narnia*. 1950–956. Reprint, New York: HarperCollins, 2017.

———. *The Problem of Pain* in *Classic of Collection*. Adage Books House, 2021 edition.

———. *The Screwtape Letters*. New York: HarperCollins, 1941.

Liebscher, Teresa, and Dawna De Silva. *SOZO Saved Healed Delivered: A Journey into Freedom with the Father, Son, and Holy Spirit*. Shippensburg, PA: Destiny Image, 2016.

Lim, David. *Spiritual Gifts: A Fresh Look*. Springfield, MO: Gospel Publishing House, 1991.

Lozano, Neal. *Unbound: A Practical Guide to Deliverance from Evil Spirits*. South Bloomington, MN: Chosen Books, 2003.

MacNutt, Francis. *Deliverance from Evil Spirits: A Practical Manual*. Grand Rapids, MI: Baker, 2009.

Maier, Paul L., translator and commentary. *Eusebius: The Church History*. Grand Rapids, MI: Kregel Academic, 1999.

Maiese, M. "Dissociative Identity Disorder and Ambivalence." *Philosophical Explorations* 19(3) (2016) 223–37.

Mangum, Doug. "Sanctification." In *The Lexham Bible Dictionary*, edited by John D. Barry et al. Bellingham, WA: Lexham, 2016.

Martin, Malachi. *Hostage to the Devil: The Possession and Exorcism of Five Contemporary Americans*. San Francisco: Harper One, 2013.

Mayes, Benjamin T. G. "Demon Possession and Exorcism in Lutheran Orthodoxy." *Concordia Theological Quarterly* 81(3–4) (2017) 331–36.

McChesney, Robert W. *The Soul Also Keeps the Score*. Collegeville, MN: Liturgical, 2025.

McGee, Gary B. *People of the Spirit: The Assemblies of God*. Rev. ed. Springfield, MO: Gospel Publishing House, 2014. Kindle.

Meier, Paul, et al. *Blue Genes*. Carol Stream, IL: Tyndale House, 2005. Kindle.

Menzies, William Alexander. *Demonic Possession in the New Testament: Its Relations Historical, Medical, and Theological*. New York: Charles Scribner's Sons, 1902.

Meza, Jose M. "Multiple Personality Disorder and Demonic Possession." PhD Diss., The Chicago School of Professional Psychology, 2010. ProQuest.

Montgomery, John Warwick. *Demon Possession: Papers Presented at the University of Notre Dame*. Athens, GA: NRP Books, 2015.

Moscicke, Hans. "The Gerasene Exorcism and Jesus' Eschatological Expulsion of Cosmic Powers: Echoes of Second Temple Scapegoat Traditions in Mark 5.1–20." *Journal for the Study of the New Testament* 41(3) (2019) 363–83.

NAMI. "Mental Illness by the Numbers." www.nami.org. Arlington, VA: National Association on Mental Illness, 2026.

Neubauer, A., trans. *Book of Tobit*. Public domain, 1878. https://www.sefaria.org/Book_of_Tobit.1.1?ven=The_Book_of_Tobit,_English_translation_by_A._Neubauer,_1878&lang=bi.

Noll, Richard. "When Psychiatry Battled the Devil." *Psychiatric Times* (2013) 1–7. http://psychiatrictimes.com.

Oliver, Jeff. *Pentecost to the Present: The Holy Spirit's Enduring Work in the Church, Book Three*. Newberry, FL: Bridge Logos, 2017.

Onyinah, Opoku. *Pentecostal Exorcism: Witchcraft and Demonology in Ghana*. Dorset, UK: Deo, 2012.

Ossa-Richardson, Anthony. "Possession or Insanity? Two Views from the Victorian Lunatic Asylum." *Journal of the History of Ideas* 74(4) (2013) 553–75.

Palilla, Benigno. *Rescued from Satan: 14 People Recount their Journey from Demonic Possession to Liberation*. Padre Pio Press, 2018.

Peck, M. Scott. *Glimpses of the Devil: A Psychiatrist's Personal Accounts of Possession, Exorcism, and Redemption*. Washington, DC: Free Press, 2005.

Quay, Mark Allen. *A Minister's Manual for Spiritual Warfare*. Eugene, OR: Resource, 2016.

Reddin, Opal. *Power Encounter: A Pentecostal Perspective*. Springfield, MO: Central Bible College Press, 1989.

Rexine, John E. "Daimon in Classical Greek Literature." *Greek Orthodox Theological Review* 30(3) (1985) 335–61.

Ripperger, Chad. *Dominion: The Nature of Diabolic Warfare*. Keenesburg, CO: Sensus Traditionist, 2022.

Roberson, John W. and M. Daniel Carrol R. *Eerdmans Commentary on the Bible: Haggai, Zechariah, Malachi*. Grand Rapids, MI: Eerdmans, 2003.

Rose, Michael S. "Diagnosing the Spectrum of Diabolic Attacks." *New Oxford Review* 88(3) (April 2021) 18–26.

Rosik, Christopher H. "Possession Phenomena in North America: A Case Study with Ethnographic, Psychodynamic, Religious and Clinical Implications." *Journal of Trauma & Dissociation* 5(1) (2004) 49–76.

Saad Asim Choudhry, Muhammad Jahanzaib Anwar, Muhammad Aadil, Ahsan Zil-e-Ali, Aitzaz Munir, Yasar Sattar, and Usama Talib. "A Case of Possession Syndrome." *International Journal of Advanced Research* 5(12) (January 2018) 542–44.

Saki, Fatemeh, and Abdoljavad Ahmadi. “Spirit Possession, Mental Suffering, and Treatment by Theurgic Flight Anthropological Study of a Culture-Bound Syndrome among the Turkmens of Iran.” *Culture & Psychology* 28(4) (2022) 567–92.

Salem, Claire Elayne. “*Sanity, Insanity, and Man's Being as Understood by St. John Chrysostom.*” PhD Diss., Durham theses, Durham University, 2010. http://etheses.dur.ac.uk/3269/.

Sands, Kathleen. *The Role of Psychological Distress and Social Contagion in Demonic Possession in Early Modern England.* History diss., University of Edinburgh, 2017.

Schaff, Philip, ed. *The Church Fathers. The Complete Ante-Nicene & Nicene and Post-Nicene Church Fathers Collection: 3 Series, 37 Volumes, 65 Authors, 1,000 Books, 18,000 Chapters, 16 Million Words.* London: Catholic Way, 2014.

Schneiders, Paul C. *Complete edition: Including Enoch 1: the Ethiopian Book of Enoch, Enoch 2: the Slavonic Secrets of Enoch, and Enoch 3: the Hebrew Book of Enoch.* Translated by R. H. Charles. Las Vegas: International Alliance Pro-Publishing, 2012.

Sersch, Michael J. *Demons on the Couch: Spirit Possession, Exorcisms and the DSM-5.* Newcastle upon Tyne, UK: Cambridge Scholars, 2019.

Seymour, William J., ed. “Testimonies of Healing.” *The Apostolic Faith* (Los Angeles, CA), February 1907.

Shelton, Brian. *Theology of a Diary: The 1949 St. Louis Exorcism.* Eugene, OR: Pickwick, 2025.

Shepherd, Jerry E. *Leviticus.* The Story of God Bible Commentary 3. Edited by Tremper Longman III and Scot McKnight. Grand Rapids, MI: Zondervan, 2021. Kindle.

Showalter, Brandon. “Witches Outnumber Presbyterians in the United States; Wicca, Paganism Growing ‘Astronomically.’” Apologetics Resource Center, 2022. https://arcapologetics.org/witches-outnumber-presbyterians-in-the-us-wicca-paganism-growing-astronomically/.

Silva, Moisés, ed. *New International Dictionary of New Testament Theology and Exegesis.* Grand Rapids, MI: Zondervan, 2014.

Smith, Ralph L. *Micah-Malachi,* Word Biblical Commentary 32. Grand Rapids, MI: Zondervan, 1984. Kindle.

Somer, Eli. “Trance Possession Disorder in Judaism: Sixteenth-Century Dybbuks in the Near East.” *Journal of Trauma & Dissociation* 5(2) (2004) 131–46.

Strong, James. *Strong's Greek and Hebrew Dictionary of the Bible.* Toronto: Toronto Publishing, 2016. Kindle.

Sutton, Geoffrey. *Counseling and Psychotherapy with Pentecostal and Charismatic Christians: Culture and Research/ Assessment and Practice.* Lithonia, GA: Sunflower, 2022. Kindle.

Swinton, John, and Angela Reed, eds. *Seeking Sanctuary, Finding Shalom: Toward a Deeper Practical Theology of Mental Health (George W. Truett Parchman Lecture Series).* Waco, TX: Baylor University Press, 2025.

Tamaş, Iosif, and Alexandra Boloş. “The Exorcism. A Religious and Medical Perspective on the Demonic-Possession Phenomenon.” *Bulletin of Integrative Psychiatry* 1 (March 2022) 97–104.

Tan, Siang-Yang. *Counseling and Psychotherapy: A Christian Perspective.* 2nd ed. Grand Rapids, MI: Baker Academic, 2022.

———. “Inner Healing Prayer.” *Christian Counseling Today* 11 (2003) 20–22.

Thomas, John Christopher. *The Devil, Disease, and Deliverance: Origins of Illness in New Testament Thought.* Cleveland, TN: CPT Press, 2012.

Trice, P. D., & Bjorck, J. P. "Pentecostal Perspectives on Causes and Cures of Depression." *Professional Psychology: Research and Practice* 37(3) (2006) 283–94.

Twelftree, Graham H. *Christ Triumphant: Exorcism Then and Now*. London: Hodden and Stoughton, 1985.

———. *In the Name of Jesus: Exorcism Among Early Christians*. Grand Rapids, MI: Baker Academic, 2007. Kindle.

Tyra, Gary. *The Dark Side of Discipleship: Why and How the New Testament Encourages Christians to Deal with the Devil*. Eugene, OR: Cascade, 2020. Kindle.

Van Der Kolk, Bessel. *The Body Keeps the Score: Brain, Mind, and Body in the Healing of Trauma*. New York: Penguin, 2015.

Van Duijl, M., et al. "Dissociative Symptoms and Reported Trauma among Patients with Spirit Possession and Matched Healthy Controls in Uganda." *Journal of Trauma and Dissociation* 14(2) (2013) 224–35.

Vaughan, Joy L. *Phenomenal Phenomena: Biblical and Multicultural Accounts of Spirits and Exorcism*. Waco, TX: Baylor University Press, 2023.

Vondey, Wolfgang. *Pentecostal Theology: Living the Full Gospel*. London: Bloomsbury T&T Clark, 2017. Kindle.

Wahlen, Clinton. *Jesus and the Impurity of Spirits in the Synoptic Gospels*. Tübingen: Mohr Siebeck, 2004.

Walton, John H., and J. Harvey Walton. *Demons and Spirits in Biblical Theology: Reading the Biblical Text in Its Cultural and Literary Context*. Eugene, OR: Cascade, 2019.

Wedderburn, Taneika. "'So What Went Into the Pigs?' Part 1 (Mark 5:1–20)." *Caribbean Journal of Evangelical Theology* 19 (2020) 64–87.

Weintraub, Collin. "'Remove These Chains!' Spiritual Possession Syndrome as an Example of Cross-Cultural Psychiatry." *Journal of the Academy of Consultation-Liaison Psychiatry* 62(6) (November/December 2021) 661–62.

Weller, Philip T., trans. *The Roman Ritual, Part 2*. Milwaukee, WI: Bruce Publishing Company, 1964.

Wenham, Gordan J. *Genesis 1–15*. Word Biblical Commentary 1. Grand Rapids, MI: Zondervan, 1987.

Whiston, William, trans. *The Works of Josephus: Complete and Unabridged*. Peabody, MA: Hendrickson, 1987.

Williams, Michael. "Not Your Average Exorcist: Jesus's Dialogue with Legion (Mark 5:7–9) in Light of Ancient Power Rituals." *Lexington Theological Quarterly* (Online) 50(1–4) (2020) 1–40.

Willis, Robert. "Liberation and Integration: Equipping Pastors to Help People Distressed by Demonic Influence Or Mental Illness." DMin diss., Assemblies of God Theological Seminary, 2025. ProQuest.

Witherington, Ben. *The Gospel of Mark: A Socio-rhetorical Commentary*. Grand Rapids, MI: Eerdmans, 2001.

Wohlgelernter, Devora K. "Death Wish in the Bible." *Tradition: A Journal of Orthodox Thought* 19(2) (1981) 131–40.

World Health Organization. *The ICD-10 Classification of Mental and Behavioral Disorders: Clinical Descriptions and Diagnostic Guidelines*. Geneva: WHO Publications, 1992.

Wright, N. T. *Jesus and the Victory of God: Volume 2: Christan Origins and the Question of God*. London: Society for Promoting Christian Knowledge, 1996. Kindle.

———. *Simply Jesus: A New Vision of Who He Was, What He Did, and Why He Matters*. San Francisco: HarperOne, 2011. Kindle.

Yap, P. M. "The Possession Syndrome: A Comparison of Hong Kong and French Findings." *American Journal of Psychotherapy* 15 (2018) 513–15.

Yong, Amos. *The Bible, Disability, and the Church: A New Vision of the People of God.* Grand Rapids, MI: Eerdmans, 2011.

York, John. *Missions in the Age of the Spirit.* Springfield, MO: Gospel Publishing House, 2000.

Young, Francis. *A History of Anglican Exorcism: Deliverance and Demonology in Church Ritual.* London: I. B. Tauris, 2018.

www.ingramcontent.com/pod-product-compliance
Lightning Source LLC
LaVergne TN
LVHW050632100826
845148LV00011B/1846